The Edward R. Murrow Heritage
CHALLENGE FOR THE FUTURE

The Edward R.

BETTY HOUCHIN WINFIELD AND
Associate Professor, Department of Communicatons

Murrow Heritage

CHALLENGE FOR THE FUTURE

LOIS B. DeFLEUR, *Washington State University*
Dean, College of Sciences and Arts

IOWA STATE UNIVERSITY PRESS / *Ames, Iowa*

Dedicated to **JANET HUNTINGTON BREWSTER MURROW**

The photographs of Edward R. Murrow used in this book are from the Historical Photograph Collection of Washington State University Libraries, Pullman, Washington. Pages: iii, 3, on set of See It Now, 1952, photo by Peter Martin (79–131); 23, preparing for See It Now broadcast, 1952 (79–132); 37, in London, 1940 (83–114); 53, in Korea, 1952 (83–124); 69, as co-producer (with Fred Friendly) of See It Now, ca. 1953 (85–038); panel photographs by James Michael Short and the staff of the Washington State University Daily Eagle.

© 1986 The Iowa State University Press. All rights reserved
Composed and printed by The Iowa State University Press, Ames, Iowa 50010

First edition, 1986

Library of Congress Cataloging-in-Publication Data
Main entry under title:

The Edward R. Murrow heritage.

Papers presented at a symposium held in 1983 at the Washington State University, Pullman, Wash.
Includes index.
1. Broadcast journalism — Congresses. 2. Murrow, Edward R. — Congresses. I. Winfield, Betty Houchin, 1939–   . II. DeFleur, Lois B., 1936–
PN4784.B75E38   1986   070.1'9   85–23874
ISBN 0–8138–1191–0

CONTENTS

PREFACE

MORE THAN EVER BEFORE the accountability of America's mass media has been questioned in how news organizations vie with each other to gather and report the news. The issues surrounding media responsibility, their rights to access information, and their demands for special professional privileges have filled court records and have been the subject of broadcast and magazine features and even films.

This book traces the impact of one person, Edward R. Murrow, and the age-old dilemma of what to say and how to say it. Yet this book is not about the past, rather it is about today and what has happened to a set of ideals about what the media could and should do. These ideas were explored in 1983 by some thirty media representatives and scholars at a symposium commemorating what would have been Murrow's seventy-fifth birthday. The symposium, "The Murrow Heritage, A Challenge for the Future," was the result of two years of hard work by the Washington State University community and particularly the members of the planning committee: William Catton, Susan Franko, Richard Hagood, Burt Harrison, Connie Kravas, Muriel Oaks, Allan Ruddy, Stanton Schmid, James VanLeuven, Kay Wilke, and the authors. So many individuals and corporations provided financial support that they are too numerous to list here, but without their contributions the symposium and this book would not have become a reality. Yet special appreciation must be given to CBS, the Haas Foundation, and the Gannett Foundation.

But, most of all, we want to thank all program participants and the faculty and students of Washington State University who grappled with and questioned many of Murrow's standards and ideals during this program. Also, two important persons who worked with us continuously during the planning period deserve special recognition: Professor Emeritus Burt Harrison and Richard Salant. For their guidance and support during the publication process we also thank Iowa State University Press, especially Suzanne Lowitt. For their extra efforts in doing the tedious production and the background research, our gratitude goes to Vicki Ambrose and most especially to Susan Cooke Anastasi.

The work on this volume was an equal endeavor and the name order was determined by a flip of a coin. Most remarkedly, we remained friends and colleagues throughout the process and have learned from our two fields.

Betty Houchin Winfield
Lois B. DeFleur

INTRODUCTION

EVERY PROFESSION HAS VISIONARIES who become legends and standard bearers. In the field of mass media, and, in particular, in broadcast journalism, that visionary was Edward R. Murrow. Although he died some twenty years ago, Murrow has continued to represent a media tradition of courage and integrity — the finest in American journalism. Murrow set the standards during each development of broadcasting from the early radio programs of the 1930s to the possibilities of satellite telecommunications during the 1960s. When World War II broke in Europe and radio reached a mass audience unmatched by any other medium, Murrow created vivid word pictures of the most dramatic and destructive events in human history. He tested his talents when television began reporting the presidential conventions, the war in Korea, and the Cold War crises of the 1950s. When the first transcontinental simultaneous broadcast was shown by a television network, Murrow was there; when the first broadcast satellite was launched, Murrow was still around. His career spanned the entire spectrum of broadcasting. Yet it was Murrow's own genius, creativity, and character that caused his significant impact, a still lingering impact, on the profession.

The evolution of American mass media, in Murrow's day, as well as today, has included numerous attempts to control news gathering and news content. Radio, television, and most recently cable and satellite technologies have been cursed as well as praised, condemned as well as complimented. Public demands on these media are often contradictory — whether the medium is used for entertainment or public affairs programs. Since Watergate, the public has become even more wary of American journalism, whether it be arrogance about their mistakes or their divisive exposés of wrongdoing, sloppy reporting, or lack of accountability. Thus, it is no surprise that the general public has not backed media pleas for special legal privileges such as confidentiality of news sources, additional access to courts and prisons, or immunity from legally warranted searches in newsrooms. These dilemmas persist and are the basis of the discussions in this book.

Started a decade ago, Washington State University's Murrow Symposium has become one of the nation's foremost platforms for airing critical issues in broadcasting and mass communications. Each symposium has been designed to challenge traditional thinking about the contemporary roles of mass media in modern society. For the 1983 symposium, some thirty prominent media personalities, executives, and scholars examined the importance of Edward R. Murrow's professional principles, substantive reporting, and standards of social responsibility for current media problems and issues. Through their discussions, trivialization was eschewed and journalistic responsibilities were reaffirmed.

There are six chapters in this volume. The first five chapters include interpretive essays connected to five symposium panel discussions. The keynote address by Diane Sawyer is Chapter six. The five essays, as critical analyses of current media issues, amplify the various themes of the panels, which have been edited to retain their salient aspects.

Speakers at the symposium included significant figures spanning the development of broadcasting as well as current media scholars. One panel included all former CBS News presidents and the then-current president Van Gordon Sauter, providing a historical perspective of the entire spectrum of television news broadcasting. That panel was moderated by Everette Dennis, Director of Columbia University's new Gannett Center for Media Studies. The panel on news, moderated by William Small, then president of United Press International, included Charles Kuralt and Joe Wershba. To discuss war coverage, then Middle Eastern correspondent Bob Faw and former war correspondent Clete Roberts were joined by Fendall Yerxa, former *New York Times* Washington Bureau chief. The then CBS morning news anchor Diane Sawyer gave the keynote address. The final session was presented as a hypothetical case study about relationships between the media and government. This exercise was directed by Fred Friendly and included scholars John Stevens and Arval Morris, Federal District Judge Robert McNichols, Washington State Attorney General Kenneth Eikenberry, Washington correspondent Barry Serafin, and others.

As noted in the edited panel discussions and amplified in the analyses, broadcast standards set by Edward R. Murrow remain the viable ideals in today's rapidly changing industry. The conflicts have increased between fulfilling the Murrow legacy of public affairs reporting and high ethical standards and economic pressures for making profits. Participants also referred to the obstacles to fulfilling the media's important social responsibilities and the public's "right to know." Among these obstacles are governmental pressures such as security and policy censorship, the media's arrogance and own self-regulation, and the various inhibitions caused by the tremendous growth of media concentration and bureaucracy.

Chapter 1 in many ways sets the stage by presenting an overview of media issues, which are covered in greater depth in subsequent chapters. "Changing Times and Changing Issues" affect reporters and media executives alike. Consequently, we briefly trace the increased concentration of media ownership and the growth of administrative bureaucracies. These changes have contributed to economic pressures that have affected the output of public-interest documentaries. In the accompanying panel discussion, current and former broadcast executives state their views about these developments and suggest possible solutions.

In Chapter 2, "The News and the Messenger: Yesterday and Today," we focus on news issues, many of which Murrow raised more than three decades ago. Still relevant are questions about how news content has been affected by recent technologies and how the ratings affect the news product and particularly the quality of news presentations. A media executive, program producer, and a reporter share their views and lament the lack of a modern-day Edward R. Murrow. They agree that Bill Moyers, more than any other broadcast figure, is a modern-day media visionary and standard bearer.

In Chapter 3, "Edward R. Murrow: The Man and the Era," we consider the important influences that affected Murrow's development as an exraordinary person and broadcaster. We review how his early family life, education, and work experiences strengthened Murrow's sense of integrity, courage, and humility. These qualities helped him achieve one success after another, altering the course of modern broadcasting.

The problems of crises coverage are the topics of Chapter 4, "The Dilemmas of War Coverage: From the London Blitz to the Beirut Battles." We analyze both the changing relationships of reporters and the military in different wars, as well as the different roles and responsibilities of journalists during these crises. Murrow's experiences in World War II as well as those recounted by our panelists illustrate the dangers of both government and reporter self-censorship.

Chapter 5, "Media, Morality and the Public," raises ethical issues such as how far should a reporter go to get a story. The analysis and the unusual panel discussion grapple with some of the dilemmas of news gathering and news reporting. This panel discussion is longer than the others because of Fred Friendly's unique format of a hypothetical case study of a national security problem. Friendly's socratic method leads the reporters, media executives, scholars, and governmental officials to some uncomfortable self-revelations.

Our last chapter is Diane Sawyer's keynote address, "A Challenge for Tomorrow." She represents the future—a new generation of television broadcasters who never knew Edward R. Murrow. Nevertheless, Diane Sawyer in her vivid and reflective style clearly states the requirements needed by those who will chronicle society's significant events. She urges reporters to put substance before style and to steep themselves in history and diverse human experiences. Warning entering journalists against becoming media personalities alone, Sawyer cautions, "celebrity corrupts and celebrity alone corrupts absolutely." Sawyer challenges television stations and networks in the future to reward intelligence, experience, and reporting skills rather than pretty faces and pleasant sounding voices. Her final words echo the legacy of the Murrow heritage; the challenge for tomorrow is where it always has been—with journalists and the depth and substance of their reporting.

The Edward R. Murrow Heritage
CHALLENGE FOR THE FUTURE

Changing Times, Changing Industry: Impact of the Murrow Heritage

> Information arises from the nature of things in themselves, and the institutions, technologies and organizational arrangements that help it travel through special space tend to impose their own natures and their own needs upon it.
>
> ANTHONY SMITH, *Goodby Gutenberg*

FROM THEIR INCEPTION, radio and television broadcasting in the United States have been largely commercial enterprises concerned with making a profit. Consequently, programmers have tended to make their decisions on the basis of audience demand, emphasizing the mass media's ability to entertain and amuse rather than educate and inform the public. These two early emphases, which gained large audiences and thus the profits, shaped the broadcast industries that exist today and obviously will influence their future development.

To what extent have changing times and changing issues affected the industry and the roles of industry executives? Our distinguished panel of five former presidents of CBS News provide perspectives covering almost half the years news broadcasting has been in existence. Their joint experience spans almost the entire spectrum of the television industry on one major network. Their discussion underscores the constant conflict between their various responsibilities of presenting news, informing the public, and meeting the organizational demands of economic survival and profit making.

The histories of radio and television reveal a parallel development. In each, the early years constituted what scholars have come to label a "golden" era (Barnouw 1968, 1970). Since their first audiences—those affluent enough to afford the new "sets"—tended to be relatively well educated, programming attempted to cater to more sophisticated tastes. Early radio documentaries like "Hear It Now," "This I Believe," and "Background" were of a uniformly high standard. So were television's early attempts at the same genre—for example, "Years of Crisis," "See It Now," and "CBS Reports." Television's early creative efforts in programs such as "Playhouse 90," "The Defenders," and "Omnibus" have also been applauded. However, as the market became saturated with radio and television sets, program standards were relaxed in an attempt to appeal to a less sophisticated general public. The lesson was there for the broadcast industry—programs do not have to be good, they simply should not be bad. As Fred Friendly said of senior management: "Their problem is that they make so much doing their worst, they cannot afford to do their best."

The nature of broadcast news also changed over the years. Initially, radio news was condensed into unsponsored five-minute reports, but during the thirties and forties news programs were extended—in part, because of the nature of world events. With so much happening, such as Franklin D. Roosevelt's New Deal, the abdication in England, the outbreak of a world war, the fall of Paris, the Battle of Britain, the shock of the Pearl Harbor bombing, the concluding peace, the American people wanted information and broadcasters tried to provide it. Whereas in 1937 only 2.8 percent of NBC's total programming hours were taken up by news, by 1944 this had increased to 26.4 percent (Emery and Emery 1978, 403).

The postwar years saw the rapid development of telecast news. In 1953 both NBC and CBS offered nightly newscasts of fifteen minutes; by 1964 the evening news had been expanded to thirty-minute presentations and now, as noted by the panel, one-hour network news is the goal. However, the news was more than just a means to satisfy the Federal Communications Commission (FCC) public affairs requirements; it became a potential for profits. Advertising time gradually increased so that by 1983 all three networks offered at least eight minutes of advertising in each thirty-minute news program. And the news itself came to be regarded as the lead-in to prime-time programming in some regions of the country. It could capture large audiences for the programs that followed.

CORPORATE MEDIA PRESSURES

The panel members repeatedly emphasize the increased pressures over time on the networks to make profits and please the affiliates. The ideal of public service by providing information for a people in a democracy has continually run into direct conflict with the realities in which today's mass media operate. Edward R. Murrow resisted compromise with purely commercial pressures as much as he could. According to Bill Leonard, Murrow once observed, "If I ran CBS, I'm afraid we'd be operating at a loss." Yet Leonard, Fred Friendly, and Richard Salant conclude that today's pressures are so great that even a Murrow would find them hard to resist.

Today's broadcast industry is an integral part of the American corporate structure in its increasing concentrations of media ownership. CBS operates a television network consisting of 210 affiliated stations and 5 stations owned by the company as well as 2 radio networks, 13 radio stations, a publishing division, a music division, and a toy division (Smith 1985, 35). Ben Bagdikian of the University of California reports that only fifty conglomerates own over half of all the nation's broadcast and print outlets and suggests that their senior management could constitute a new private Ministry of Information and Culture (Bagdikian 1983, xvi, 3–103).

Yet the traditional role of mass media in a democracy is based on the assumption that there are many viewpoints and ideas from which to choose. Various commissions on press freedom, even the Supreme Court, have referred to the ideal of a marketplace of multiple ideas in which, in John Milton's classic formulation, "(truth) and falsehood grapple; whoever knew Truth put to the worse in a free and open encounter?" (1951, 50). During Murrow's day, the Commission on Freedom of the Press emphatically stated that the loss of the mass media marketplace would be the greatest possible threat to the liberty of expression in a democracy. In their 1947 report (15–16), the commission warned:

The right of free public expression has lost its earlier reality. Protection against government is now not enough to guarantee that a man who has something to say shall have a chance to say it. The owners and managers of the press determine which person, which facts, which version of the facts and which ideals shall reach the people.

This ideal of a multitude of voices in the marketplace was also maintained by the Supreme Court during the tenure of several of the panelists. In one famous libel case the court cited both Milton and John Stuart Mill in support of the assertion that an idea, even a false one (so long as it is not a calculated falsehood), meets First Amendment protection when the communication at issue involves criticism of elected government officials (*New York Times v. Sullivan*). The Court also used the marketplace concept as justification for upholding the broadcast fairness doctrine in 1969, emphasizing the importance of public debate by requiring that networks give free time to opposing viewpoints on significant public issues (*Red Lion Broadcasting v. FCC*). Furthermore, the Court stressed that broadcast stations must produce diverse programming and that their licensing must be in the public interest.

The recent introduction and rapid expansion of cable systems have greatly complicated the application of the fairness doctrine. While the FCC regulates the ownership structure of the broadcast industry (a single industry cannot own more than twelve television stations and twelve AM or twelve FM radio stations or less than 25 percent of the market, effective

April 1985), the commission has very few controls over cable. There is no ownership limitation on pay-cable distribution, nor is there a limit on the number of channels a company may control. As a result, companies that own cable systems, such as Time, Incorporated, and Teleprompter, may provide their own transmission facilities as well as their own programming. Under such conditions, as Christopher Sterling noted, cable systems may "accomplish what the broadcast networks have been prohibited from doing, controlling the distribution as well as the content. . . . In just half a decade, the economic future of pay cable has become a game only giants can play" (Sterling 1979, 314–15).

Panelist Richard Salant, former vice-chairman and senior adviser to NBC, notes that "for better or worse, this country has chosen to have its broadcast organization a free, competitive private enterprise." But under such a system a conglomerate like Time, Incorporated, has come to control about 80 percent of pay-cable distribution. Some observers ask whether the marketplace concept is perhaps out of sync with the reality of today's conglomerate media market.

By regulation, the FCC does try to keep the ideal of a multiplicity of voices alive by encouraging minority ownership of broadcasting stations with preference licensing and favorable tax treatment and also by encouraging minority cable ownership. Congress, too, has made efforts by citing the necessary function of newspapers as an educational and information service to justify the Newspaper Preservation Act in 1970. But despite these efforts, media ownership is being relentlessly consolidated. Even a decade ago, daily newspapers owned one-fourth of all the country's television stations and 34 percent of all TV revenues; newspapers also owned 250 AM radio stations serving one-third of the American population, and had 80 percent of the top three radio markets (Bagdikian 1971, 174–75). Today, the major television networks control program production and network distribution and reach huge markets (25–30 percent of all television homes); in fact, among the 100 top media companies in the country, the three leaders in media sales are ABC, CBS, and RCA Corporation, which owns NBC ("100 Leading Media Companies" 1981, S-3).

As our panelists note, the growth of these corporations and their accompanying bureaucracies intensifies profit pressures and strongly influences policy decisions and program content. The trend is toward more gossip, shock, and scandal in an attempt to gain the highest ratings. Hence the maximum profit may speak for itself.

THE CHANGING ROLE OF MEDIA DECISION MAKERS

In less than four decades, CBS under William Paley grew from a small, foundering New York based radio network to a $3 billion a year communications empire. It, like the other networks, now has numerous divisions, sections, stations, and operating units that include equally diverse person-nel — presidents, vice-presidents, executive producers, programmers, station managers, ad infinitum. The roles of media executives have changed as can be noted in the comments of the panelists.

Edward R. Murrow held an executive post with CBS just after the war when its bureaucratic growth was beginning; he too felt the effects. In 1945 he returned from Europe, his friendship with William Paley firmly es-tablished. Paley wanted to appoint Murrow to a fitting role that reflected his new-found prominence as a newscaster and decided that Murrow's crea-tive talents and high standards might be best used in news programming and staff development. Murrow reluctantly agreed and in 1946 became vice-president and director of public affairs. He did his job energetically and enthusiastically and within a short time had introduced a different variety of news programming.

He established a news documentary unit whose first assignment was the postwar role of Germany. Programs he put on the network included "As Others See Us," a program dealing with foreign comment on the United States, and "CBS Was There," which later became "You Are There," a pop-ular historical events program. Besides "The Morning News Roundup," Murrow instituted a fifteen-minute daily program linking American cities. But the show in which he took the keenest interest was "CBS Views the Press," a controversial program that he intended as a critical and objective analysis of the press. With these programs, Murrow had a direct innovative impact on the form and content of media programming. While this was a source of great satisfaction to him, he was happiest when he was in the studio working with producers and broadcasters. Paley and others sensed that Murrow's heart was not in his job, and after a brief eighteen months, Murrow resigned this post to return to broadcasting.

Murrow's unhappiness stemmed in part from his frustration over the increasing separation of creative and administrative functions. As the network grew in size and complexity, the organizational separation in-creased and, as Fred Friendly and other panelists suggested, this has led to an intensification of executive frustration. Such complexity made it diffi-cult, if not impossible, either to assume or to attribute responsibility for decisions.

Most of the problems faced by executives stem from the ever-present tension between the need to fulfill the media's mandate to provide pro-gramming in the public interest and the desire to make profits. As our panelists point out, many of the most significant programs offered by the networks, even the award-winning Murrow documentaries, have not been successful in drawing audiences and making profits. Fred Friendly summa-rized it best: "When they say it's not the money, it's the money."

As a result of economic competition from cable systems and other new technologies, executives assert that the tension becomes more difficult to resolve. Corporate interest wins out ever more frequently over public in-terest. "In Nielson We Trust" as a motto is but a symbol of the competitive pressures. Sig Mickelson, who was president of CBS News twenty-five years ago, notes that the pressures for higher ratings are centered at senior management levels as well as with affiliates. The real dilemma is how to get the ratings without distorting the product. The pressures have become so intense that programming integrity is threatened. Other panelists agreed, all recognizing that there are no easy answers to these persistent and complex issues. Perhaps one consequence of the insolubility of these dilemmas is the rapid turnover of media executives. Networks are constantly searching for the "right" executives to help them in the battle for ratings.

Who are these powerful right executives? How do they meet the demands made of them? Are they innovators and agenda setters, or are they managers and administrators? Not surprisingly, the administrative philosophy and personal style of media executives vary considerably. For example, a recent interview with Roone Arledge, president of ABC, reveals his style and the way in which he approaches problems of programming and profits (Collins 1983, 21):

"I'm a different kind of administrator. I pick the very best people around me, and I delegate things. I encourage a free-form work atmosphere, but you can't have a good organization without discipline. You've got to have rules, but when you find a better way to do something, if the situation allows you to do something better, then you've got to break the rules. . . . The bottom line is that everything gets done. We operate at a profit."

In many ways, Arledge's approach is no different from that of most Wall Street or Madison Avenue executives. Arledge has been labeled "the most influential figure in TV news and sports" (Collins 1983, 16).

A somewhat different style, also effective, characterizes CBS's Van Sauter. His roots are in print media as he spent a number of years as a reporter in Chicago before he joined the network. During his tenure with CBS, he has held many different jobs in different areas, in both sports and news. His style is distinctive (Kitman 1982, 27):

Van feels, as president of news, his most imporant job is to oversee these things personally. The CBS Evening News is the network's front page, and Van Sauter sees himself as its editor as well as the publisher. His vision of the job was that he should get in there, roll up his sleeves and make over the front page.

This "hands-on" approach seems to suit Sauter and seems to work for him, but his goals are the same as other media executives. Profits are important and the ratings must be heeded, but some attention must be given to values such as accountability and social responsibility. Although he had worked for CBS for fifteen years and had never been given a specific mandate, he summarized these network values during a recent interview:

Do you want ratings? Revenue? Profit? Community Service? Image? What do you want from that television station? Mr. Paley was said to have replied, "I want all those things." That's what I've assumed to be the mandate-never-spoken from CBS.

"Wanting it all" is indeed the bottom line and the root of the dilemma of all media executives. How they manage to resolve it depends on their personal style and values. Murrow, in his brief tenure as executive, apparently had some successes, but during those embryonic days of television he faced a far less complex situation. Today, the future of American broadcasting depends on the choices made by these executives, on their ability to reconcile profit and integrity, on their courage to choose the long-term benefits of public responsibility over the short-term benefits of seasonal ratings success. The transmission of truthful and accurate information remains as the ideal embodied in the Murrow heritage.

PANEL PARTICIPANTS

EVERETTE DENNIS *(moderator)* serves as director of the Gannett Center for Media Studies at Columbia University. Formerly, he was dean of the School of Journalism at the University of Oregon. He has authored or edited eight books on mass communication and was the 1983–1984 president of the National Association for Education in Journalism and Mass Communication.

FRED FRIENDLY is the Edward R. Murrow Professor Emeritus at the Columbia University Graduate School of Journalism and Director of the Columbia University Seminars on Media and Society. He collaborated with Murrow on the CBS radio series "Hear It Now" and the television series "See It Now." Friendly ended his network career with two years as president of CBS News. He resigned in 1966 to join the faculty at Columbia and to become a consultant to the Ford Foundation.

WILLIAM LEONARD served as president of CBS News from 1979–1982, when he retired after thirty-seven years with CBS as broadcaster, producer, and executive. He was head of the CBS News Election Unit and vice-president in charge of Public Affairs Broadcasts. Since his retirement, Leonard has been a consultant to CBS.

SIG MICKELSON was CBS's chief executive for news and public affairs from 1951–1961. He also served as vice-president of Time, Incorporated; chairman of the Editorial Department, Northwestern University; president of Radio Free Europe; and executive director of the Center for Communications, San Diego State University.

RICHARD SALANT is senior adviser to NBC and a former vice-chairman of NBC. He was twice president of CBS News (from 1961–1964 and 1966–1979) and served as vice-president of Corporate Affairs. Salant holds the LL.B. degree from Harvard.

VAN GORDON SAUTER is executive vice-president of CBS Broadcasting. During his fifteen years with CBS he has been president of CBS News, chief of the network's Paris bureau, vice-president for Network Program Practices, and president of CBS Sports. Prior to joining CBS, Sauter was a Vietnam correspondent for the *Detroit Free Press*.

We will begin by reflecting on what the Murrow heritage is and how it has impacted the changing industry and issues.
—EVERETTE DENNIS

Everette Dennis: This is a historic occasion today because it is the first time ever that all of the people who have held the title president of CBS News since Edward R. Murrow was in the post are assembled at one place, at one time. That is a remarkable achievement in and of itself. It is best to say, as someone did not long ago, that presidents of CBS News are like Olympian figures, "they're unusual in an age of faceless men and women in American business because they are very visible people." They are the managers and directors of media organizations as well as significant figures in American life. Today, we have the opportunity to explore a great deal of the history of broadcast news in this country and the values and the things that have made it great. If we were to omit the information that these men have accumulated from the history of broadcast news in America, we would have a very fragmented and incomplete picture. We will begin by reflecting on what the Murrow heritage is and how it has impacted the changing industry and issues.

The Murrow heritage is almost totally indefinable.
—SIG MICKELSON

Sig Mickelson: The Murrow heritage is almost totally indefinable. This indefinable character Murrow imparted to the CBS organization probably came from integrity. You can go through the whole list of clichés, they are all there, but it is intelligence, honesty, integrity, sympathy for the public, and a desire for high quality, or excellence.

Thirty years ago it was almost impossible to make a decision without wondering what Ed Murrow would think of the decision. In hiring, you almost invariably hired on the basis of whether or not this person was capable of measuring up to the quality and standards that Ed Murrow had established. From the point of view of broadcasting, there was the heritage for doing solid reporting, not simply rewriting off the wires. Out of all of this came a spirit and a feeling that permeated the whole organization and motivated us to keep up standards which would appeal to Murrow. There was always that question of whether or not Murrow would approve. If the answer was affirmative, then we went ahead and did it.

A president of the United States once said, "We come by our miracles easier than we are able to manage them."

—FRED FRIENDLY

Fred Friendly: I think Ed was the first user of the thousand-pound pencil. That is a term of the art that we used to use and it comes home to me when I see that miniaturized equipment out there. If Ed had been born a hundred years earlier, he would have worked with a pad and a pencil, as journalists have since Gutenberg. He came at a time when it wasn't a one-ounce pencil but a thousand pounds of equipment that Ed had to take to Korea for each cameraman: storage batteries, hundred-pound tripod. We're now halfway into that revolution, from the thousand-pound pencil to include a day not far from now when it may not be a one-ounce pencil but it won't be as large as the microphones that Ed used when he said, "This is London." We have made great technological advances. A president of the United States once said, "We come by our miracles easier than we are able to manage them."

As we move through this great technological revolution, cameras get smaller, tape recorders get smaller, and satellites become more prevalent. Mr. Van Sauter can push a button and tomorrow night we will be listening to people from all over the world in a debate on disarmament. All that technology is magnificent, but are we ever going to be able to recapture what Ed had? The people who use this technology are in many ways just as capable but the responsibility for it is spread so far.

Even though Murrow ceased to be an executive at CBS, he was always the reporter, gatekeeper, and agenda setter. I only hope that as the new generation of broadcast journalists move into executive positions, the ability to involve the audience is not lost in the contraptions and the equipment and the financial enterprise that are so essential to the survival of this business.

Everette Dennis: Dick Salant, you became president of CBS News toward the end of Ed Murrow's time there. Last night I heard you say that you were a little scared taking up that role as the head of CBS News, given this tremendous reputation, the ratings, and everything else that CBS had going for it at that time. With regard to sustaining Murrow's practices and heritage, could you tell us about that?

As new problems and new circumstances arise in this very, very difficult craft of journalism, what would Ed Murrow have done and what would he have said?
—RICHARD SALANT

Richard Salant: When senior management at CBS designated me as head of the news division I had no credentials, no qualifications, no experience. I had been an editor of my prep school paper and an editor of the *Harvard Law Review*, where our sole purpose in life was to see who could write the longest footnote. Those things hardly qualified me for this immense job of being responsible for what I regarded then, and I regard now, as the finest news organization in the country.

This panel is engaged in a very delicate and in some senses, a very dangerous inquiry. We are trying to ask ourselves, "As new problems and new circumstances arise in this very, very difficult craft of journalism, what would Ed Murrow have done and what would he have said?" But we ought to recognize things have changed and that the question is a valid question only in terms of integrity, honesty, seriousness of purpose, because there are things that were acceptable and proper in Ed's day that some of us would object to today. There are also things we are doing today that we think are acceptable that Murrow would have found unacceptable.

Everette Dennis: Bill Leonard, what happened during your time at "CBS News?" How do you reflect on Ed Murrow's standards and the changes that have taken place?

William Leonard: Broadcasting as we know it today, including CBS News, is a result of a series of fortuitous accidents of decisions and half decisions in the hands of a few remarkable people. Perhaps the most important is the man who retired only yesterday as chairman of CBS, William Paley. When

Broadcasting . . . is a result of a series
of fortuitous accidents of decisions
and half decisions in the hands
of a few remarkable people.
—WILLIAM LEONARD

Paley was trying to find out what broadcasting was all about, he soon decided that disseminating information was part of his responsibility. Somebody told him that he ought to have somebody in his shop who had some professional background. By a series of the most offhand accidents, he hired a young man from the *New York Times*, Ed Klauber, a man who was a purist in journalistic terms. Klauber had his own standards and they were tough and he hired people who were tough. Mr. Paley told me a few years ago: "Everything I learned about news at the beginning was from Klauber. We have to be fair, we have to be straight down the middle, we have to maintain our social responsibilities."

Everette Dennis: Van Sauter, the *New York Times* tells us that in your ten-month tenure you have done more to change CBS News than all of your predecessors. How about that?

. . . although the majority of the people in
our evening newsroom are in their late
thirties or early forties, there is a tremendous
sense of Murrow being there.
—VAN GORDON SAUTER

Van Gordon Sauter: I speak for a different generation of broadcast executives than my colleagues here and probably a far more dispassionate one. I look over my shoulder only fleetingly, I must say, and in terms of my relationship with my job and in what I think is a radically new broadcast news environment from the one that existed even four or five years ago. This environment has been influenced by the Murrow heritage.

It goes without saying that my associates here at this table have kept that tradition alive at CBS News for more than two decades. Indeed, although the majority of the people in our evening newsroom are in their late thirties or early forties, there is a tremendous sense of Murrow being there. In a peculiar kind of way, though, it is not addressed and it is not articulated. A great deal of what we do is done in a subliminal frame of reference of accountability. That accountability is not to me and it's not to Mr. Paley; it's fundamentally to the tradition and the excellence that has been established.

Everette Dennis: I am told that at least one of the men on this panel has on his desk a sign that says, "In Nielson We Trust." Are these goals of a profit-centered news and the kind of standards and values you all talk about compatible?

Richard Salant: We tend to exaggerate the conflict between the economics and social responsibilities. The fact is, for better or worse, this country has chosen to have its broadcast organization a free, competitive private enterprise. Outside of Germany, perhaps we are the only ones. That carries with it tensions, but it does mean that if you do not have an audience, you cannot go on. The only question is how far do you go to get the audience? That is where the legitimate debate is.

William Leonard: The television industry and the news are bigger, but news has gone from a loss leader to a profit center. News has changed from a part of the business that fought, usually unsuccessfully, for a tiny bit of prime time, for a tiny bit of exposure, for a tiny bit of money to an absolutely integral part of television. In half of the television stations in this country, almost all the difference between profit and loss is the profitability of news operation. The single most popular, most profitable series in the entire history of television is not an entertainment program as such, but a product of CBS News, "60 Minutes."

Sig Mickelson: There isn't the slightest doubt that "60 Minutes" is a lineal descendant of Murrow's "See It Now." The original "See It Now" usually tried to do about three segments in a half-hour, we now have three segments in an hour. It is essentially the same interview technique and it is the same support for the underdog, the same general attitude that you find now in "60 Minutes."

The point to make here is the question of ratings and the impact they have on the attitudes of management. It is not as serious at the network level although I say that with some trepidation because after the rise of Huntley and Brinkley, CBS spent five years trying to catch up with NBC. As a result there was a serious problem in the news division. It was not so much within the division but from some members of senior management with whom we had to get along in order to get the resources to be able to go out and do a job. It was pressure from affiliates. The affiliates were pressing the management, the management was pressing us. They wanted ratings and there was not much discussion about how to get the ratings, just get them. Now, we came up with a philosophy which I think is still applicable. That is, let's get the maximum ratings we can while still maintaining a maximum degree of integrity. In other words, not permit the desire for ratings to distort the product. I am seriously afraid that in the local station markets right now distortion is occurring. We built a fairly solid foundation in the beginning of television news for news personnel who could move into station positions with the same degree of integrity that we tried to maintain at the network level. I just don't think it is there anymore. Station managers and station owners have found that the almighty dollar is tied inexorably to ratings and they're out for those ratings.

I come back again to the fact that I do not think we ought to say quite so glibly that everybody in this business is so high minded. Their purpose isn't to support the public; rather they are paying too much attention to ratings and the profit and loss statements that go along with increased ratings.

Fred Friendly: Much of television is a game, a pinball machine done electronically. I have nothing but a sense of awe for the people who work in broadcast journalism at the networks today. Their problem is that they make so much money doing their worst they cannot afford to do their best. And, their best is only very good. Bill Leonard talks about the highest ratings show in the history of television, "60 Minutes," and that's fine. I do not want to beat up on "60 Minutes" but compare these stories to those that Murrow reported on — "Radulovich," "McCarthy," "Annie Lee Moss," "Harvest of Shame" — you can click off another thirty, forty. With the exception of one fine broadcast on "60 Minutes" seven or eight years ago done by Joe Wershba on the Tonkin Gulf, it is hard for me to remember a single broadcast of "60 Minutes" that played an important part in making the American people think hard about a complex issue. It is a very successful program, I watch it and I enjoy it, but it isn't what Murrow did. It prides itself first on the audience and the revenues and then on the programs.

The endangered species at all the networks is the documentary. You cannot do everything in twelve or thirteen minutes. Ed and his colleagues had a half hour, once a week, thirty-nine weeks a year to do what they wanted without regard for ratings.

I have, as Senator McCarthy used to say, a document, the budget for the first "See It Now" series, 7 August 1951. I wrote it. I always underestimated costs then and I still do. Cameramen: two at $250; lighting: $150; tape: $50; studio facilities and telecines: $1625; and so forth. The bottom line for a half-hour program that ran for five years was $10,349. One commercial half-minute on "60 Minutes" sells for ten times that amount and you can't do anything for $10,000.

If Murrow were alive today and he really is here today, he is in that newsroom as Sauter says, Ed would not have that half-hour of time. If Ed wanted to, he would walk into the lobby of 485 Madison Avenue and ask his associate producer to read a story from Detroit. It was a little box from the *Detroit Free Press* about an air force lieutenant, Milo Radulovich, who was being kicked out of the air force because of his family. Ed wanted to do that story. Joe Wershba was in Dexter, Michigan, that night and five or six days later that program, because it was Ed's decision, was on the air for a half-hour. It has nothing to do with the intentions, the quality, or the qualifications of any of these fine men and women who do their jobs here and at other places. No one will ever have the opportunity that Murrow had. There is somebody who has a plaque on his wall that says, "The test of television will be when it becomes a profit center." It *is* a profit center, and the testing is now.

Van Gordon Sauter: Competition is absolutely crucial at this stage in the evolution of broadcast journalism. The basic truth is that network news is an incredibly costly operation and not a profitable one. Cost increases far exceed the revenue increases. Television news, at the network level, is faced with performing its task consistent with its revenue sources. We do not want to get out of focus here and describe network television news as profit centers, because they are not. To a great degree, their license is directly dependent upon the attitude of the individuals who run the corporations that embrace them. While the network news organizations are having severe problems in terms of time available for broadcasting, and also in terms of meeting budgetary realities, local news stations are expanding their time and dramatically increasing their audiences. For every hour of network news time that is viewed, local news is viewed 1.9 hours; local news is increasingly defining what television news is.

I made a list of how times have changed and the problems facing television journalism today. One problem is local news. One can go across this country and probably only find seven or eight stations where resources are allocated, skilled people are hired, and a quality product is produced. A significant number of local television news operations are not distinguished. Probably they are no less distinguished than the local newspaper, which is not a consolation prize, but it is the reality of the communications business. One of the key problems of our industry today is to find a way to upgrade the quality of local news. Local news is defining, to a great degree, what news is and this is a serious problem and challenge.

Richard Salant: We are part of a free competitive enterprise business system. The only legitimate question which takes more thought than it does eloquence is what *don't* you do because you are part of the system? We have enormous responsibilities and how our democratic society works is dependent on how we fulfill our responsibilities in broadcast news.

William Leonard: Let's get back to Ed Murrow. Ed said, "If I ran CBS, I'm afraid we'd be operating at a loss." There's nothing Ed said that indicated he was happy with the broadcasting system devoted primarily to entertainment, primarily to making a profit. If he was unhappy then, which he was and which eventually led to his departure from CBS, he would be ten times as unhappy today. There is not much we can do about that except to keep the news as good and as close to the Murrow tradition as we can.

Sig Mickelson: I have the feeling, perhaps wrongly, that there is a tendency to condone backsliding in the interests of building up financial support to the point where we can guarantee some independence. Also, because Bill

Leonard says there are some pretty miserable conditions under which journalists work in other parts of the world should not permit us to make the assumption that we are better than others and therefore doing well. That bothers me and it bothers me also that we make too many concessions.

The networks generally have done very, very well in most cases, but I can cite at least one example that has not been given any publicity. In 1960 we had some grandiose plans for CBS Reports. The first year we had a budget put together by Bell and Howell and Goodrich. It had to run for eight programs the first year. It was tremendously successful and the next year we were going to expand them. The television network did not like the idea of this serious program interrupting its excellent nighttime schedule of hillbillies and sordid comedies in Vermont. So what the television network did was to say, "All right, we will take your figure and we will put a substantial network profit on this. We will offer it for sale at X number of dollars." Now I am sure the network's attitude was that the price was so high there wasn't a chance in the world that anybody would buy it. Therefore, the network would have that hour of time back again, which they could sell for entertaining commercial programs that yield a good profit.

Everette Dennis: Coming back again to the present, there are a number of critics who talk about contemporary television, not just CBS, but some of the other networks as well, as being more concerned with image and flash, electronic tricks. They ask whether it is journalism or literature. One critic talks in terms of CBS News, following something he calls "a theory of moments": stories that touch people, that stir feelings, stories about Princess Diana and her baby, as opposed to the Middle East. Is that an accurate characterization?

Van Gordon Sauter: I guess there is no way I can get out of this. Has television news changed a great deal over the last five years? Has CBS News changed dramatically over the last fourteen months? Has the quality of the journalism diminished? I would say not at all. In some circumstances I would say it has improved not because of my role, but because of other circumstances. Is it a broadcast that is more pertinent to life as it is lived in this society? I would say yes.

As I become involved in the discussions and the heated debates within my institution, I realize that the decision-making process has been enlarged and widened, more people are involved in the process. There are disagreements about the nature of broadcasts but I think that's constructive and valuable. There are changes taking place in network evening news today at all three networks, and the differences are at all three networks.

Is any of this inconsistent with the Murrow philosophy and attitude? I am not a person who can speak firsthand, but I do not think so. Murrow embraced the totality of human experience and I think it is important that our broadcasts do that if we are going to reach, engage, inform, and enlighten our viewers.

Fred Friendly: If the CBS Evening News were an hour long, as everybody at this table I'm sure believes it should be, there would be a place for the likes of Murrow. It is a battle that everybody at this table has fought, for the hour news to come back in 1983 and the answer is that the affiliates won't carry it. Why won't the affiliates carry it? Because most affiliates, with a few exceptions, feel that the revenue they get for doing local news, not very well, gives them no reason for carrying network news, which does a job of reporting a complex world very well.

There is a Murrow memo, written when he was at the United States Information Agency, and I was still at CBS, in which he recommends an hour nightly program doing one or two subjects in depth. This memo, written in 1963 or 1964, is a perfect definition of McNeil-Lehrer. McNeil-Lehrer fighting for public television's place, doing an hour of news that CBS, NBC, and ABC are incapable of doing because of their format. A former president of CBS News, who shall be nameless, once said, "Fred, when they say it's not the money, it's the money."

Richard Salant: I have been fighting this battle since we went from fifteen minutes to half an hour. There is nothing that the affiliates can do. There is nothing that FCC and its absurd prime-time access rules can do to stop the networks from going to an hour from eight to nine in the evening. So there are lots of villains, not only the affiliates. I think we ought to keep that in mind because we keep on fighting only the covert enemy on this, but the network still has three nice hours there between eight and eleven. I happen to think that an hour of news each night might be more valuable and might even yield greater profits than some of the things you see between eight and eleven at night on the networks.

William Leonard: Dick, I certainly do not want to put myself in the position of defending the CBS television network but I will at least give you the argument. They would tell you that you are absolutely naive to think that it is possible to devote an eight-to-nine hour to an information program. Consideration has been given to putting "60 Minutes" in an eight-to-nine period but the feeling is that "60 Minutes" could not survive against a real entertainment schedule. I do not want to get into why "60 Minutes" is okay at seven o'clock; the fact is, they cannot schedule entertainment against "60 Minutes," only children's programming or public service programming. The battle for domination of the prime-time schedule is economic, of course, but beyond that it is a battle of prestige, it's a battle for Number 1. They simply cannot take a chance, or feel they cannot.

Sig Mickelson: Bill, if you were at NBC, and NBC was running a poor third in the ratings battle, and you really wanted to battle back against ABC and CBS for supremacy somewhere between eight and eleven, wouldn't it make sense to lead with your news? You have a good news department, the cost is relatively slight, the profit margin substantial, and the prestige which would go along with it could be a significant factor in bringing NBC back up again.

William Leonard: The argument of the people at NBC would be, "Hell, what we need is an entertainment blockbuster, not a news loser."

Richard Salant: Ed Murrow would have voted to try it from eight to nine.

William Leonard: Of course he would, and of course, everybody in this row would try it from eight to nine.

Sig Mickelson: Would you try it?

Richard Salant: Well, I hope so.

Van Gordon Sauter: Let me be a dissenter. I am not convinced that I would program news for eight to nine if it was my only access to the national audience at the evening hour. The ratings would be catastrophic, the total number of people we would reach would be dramatically reduced.

Fred Friendly: How many millions do you think you would have? To the nearest million?

Van Gordon Sauter: In terms of a rating point?

Fred Friendly: Dan Rather, every night at nine o'clock says, "Good evening. This is Dan Rather. This is the 'CBS Evening News.' " One hour. How many people would be watching that?

Van Gordon Sauter: The evening news now gets around a 14.5 in terms of a rating. I obviously would have to go back to the books and talk to some of the research people but I think if we began that broadcast at eight, I don't think we would average more than a 6 or 7 rating.

Fred Friendly: Translate that into millions for us.

Van Gordon Sauter: A 14 rating would represent approximately 11 to 12 million households.

Fred Friendly: Disaster.

Van Gordon Sauter: Fred, to me it would be an absolute disaster; the millions of dollars that would be lost weekly to sustain the CBS news organization would be catastrophic. On top of that, the additional cost of enlarging the news by half an hour at a time when your revenue base would be sharply depressed would be, given the resources available, an absolute disaster. So I sit here and say I am not convinced it would be a wise move for CBS News to do news between eight and nine. The Dan Rather news is the best and I am not going to give up my audience between seven and eight or six and seven in the evening to two competitors I think do an inferior job so I can go to eight o'clock at night, get fewer people, have fewer income sources for the totality of my news organization, and to make a point. It's crazy.

Fred Friendly: Dick, you believe in an hour of nightly news.

Richard Salant: Of course I believe in it. Who doesn't believe in an hour of nightly news?

Anybody that insists it stay from six-thirty to seven-thirty or seven to eight does not really want an hour of news because he is not going to get it there. The point I'm trying to make is that if it is as important as I think we all agree it is, and it is so important because of the enormous reliance of the American public on television news, and because information is the linchpin of a working democracy, that if you cannot get the hour anywhere else, you ought to look somewhere where you have it within your own control.

Van Gordon Sauter: Dick, the price you end up paying for doing it at that stage does not justify. . . .

Richard Salant: But, Van, you were talking about, and I quote, "losing my audience." I'm talking about making democracy work and our obligations to the public. I do not think your audience belongs to you.

Van Gordon Sauter: That is a marvelous attitude to have but I will tell you right now the people who normally watch news, as is their history and their custom, will continue to watch NBC or ABC News between seven and eight, and when eight o'clock rolls around they will be watching entertainment like "The A Team."

The ultimate answer to the one-hour news, and it is not the best answer, but I think it's the only course we're going to be able to follow, is to enter into a relationship with some of the major affiliates in the top fifty market whereby our hour is structured in such a way that they have a participation in the second half-hour. Speaking realistically, that is the only way we are going to be able to expand our broadcast. The total expansion of all this would not be a half-hour, it would be fifteen minutes and that is the most constructive, positive step we could take, one that best serves our audience.

William Leonard: We tried that two and a half years ago and we couldn't sell it, but maybe down the road you will be able to sell it.

Van Gordon Sauter: "Nightline" is an outstanding broadcast; it is a marvelous idea which has done more to mature the image of ABC News than any other thing. It is a major contributor to their maturity in the network news business. The basic problem is that the "Nightline" viewer leaves television at midnight, therefore, the one-hour period between twelve and one o'clock does terribly in the ratings. The commercial potential of that ninety-minute time period is significantly reduced, which is why ABC brought on "The Last Word," a terrible show that failed justifiably. Now they are trying to fill out that period by lengthening "Nightline" and an introduction of yet a new half-hour broadcast. Their purpose is to try to get the news viewer to stay for the full ninety minutes. Unless they can do that, the broadcast will be a tremendous asset to ABC News but a tremendous liability to the rest of the broadcast organization.

Everette Dennis: In closing, I want to call on Fred Friendly, who has a quote from Ed Murrow.

Fred Friendly: In his 1958 speech to Radio/Television News Directors, Murrow said, "I do not advocate that we turn television into a twenty-seven-inch Wailing Wall where long hairs constantly moan about the state of our culture and our defense. But I would like to see it reflect occasionally the hard unyielding realities of the world in which we live. I would like to see it done inside the exciting framework of commercial television, and I would like to see the doing of it redound to the credit of those who finance and program it. Measure the results by Nielsen, Trendex, or Silex; it doesn't matter. The main thing is to try. The responsibility can be easily placed, in spite of all the mouthings about giving the public what it wants. It rests on big business and big television and it rests at the top. Responsibility is not something that can be assigned or delegated, and it promises its own reward — good business and good television."

News and the Messenger: Yesterday and Today

The speed of communication is wondrous to behold. It is also true that the speed can multiply the distribution of information that we know to be untrue. The most sophisticated satellite has no conscience. The newest computer can merely compound, at speed, the oldest problem in the relations between human beings, and in the end the communicator will be confronted with the old problem of what to say and how to say it.

EDWARD R. MURROW
Upon accepting the
Family of Man Award,
October 1964

IT HAS BEEN almost two decades since Edward R. Murrow voiced his concerns about news form and content, journalistic integrity, and professionalism. Clearly, his misgivings are still relevant today. His distress was not unique; similar issues have been raised since the inception of broadcasting in this country. And they are the focus of the following panel discussion addressing the ways in which information is affected by technology, how information becomes news, and what determines the quality of its presentation.

The panel participants—an executive, a producer, and a reporter— offer a wide range of opinions based on their own experiences during the years since the Murrow era, years during which the use of communications satellites, computers, and cable systems have led to the development of a worldwide system of communications. Today, news and entertainment can potentially be broadcast, or messages can be sent, from and to almost anywhere in the world. As newer informational technologies develop and media bureaucracies grow bigger and more complex, we are justified in asking whether the problems identified by Murrow are becoming more acute.

IMPACT OF TECHNOLOGY

Murrow once said that although the instrument can teach, illuminate, and even inspire, it can do so only to the extent that humans are determined to use it to those ends. Otherwise, he said, television is merely wires and lights in a box (Bliss 1967, 364). Murrow, who experimented with each new technological change from the first radio news roundup to television video tapes, asked whether the citizen would prefer television news to that of radio and print (Murrow 1949, 7). He predicted that television news from a studio would never have either the speed and flexibility of radio or the ability to treat major news stories in enough detail to rival print. He warned that if television news was ever to be more than a picture supplement, it must indeed put the *news*, not the picture, first (Murrow 1949, 3). It must recognize that news is primarily made up of what goes on in men's minds, reflected in their words, rather than of pictorial images of events.

The panel addresses some of the problems that have followed innovations in communications technology. The sheer speed with which information becomes available nationwide has led, for example, to the question of whether or not network voter projections have a deleterious effect on the democratic system.

Panel leader William Small offers a generally positive analysis of the effects of technology citing, for example, the thousands of research hours saved by computers. He does, however, express concern that the emphasis on speed of communication encourages only a superficial consideration of events and their context, and that the expense of the new equipment restricts the geographical areas in which it can be used. Other panelists, such as Charles Kuralt, share Small's positive view of technological advances, seeing only the advantages of speed and ease and rejecting the claim that the use of technology can raise ethical problems. Joe Wershba, on the other hand, cites Murrow's own anguish over his use of technology in the McCarthy program in 1954: "What right did I have to use all this equipment to go against one man, or to make a point of view?"

Recently, scholar James Carey, dean of the College of Communications, University of Illinois, pointed out the obvious contradiction whereby vast improvements in telecommunications through a worldwide, linked communications system of cable, computer, and satellite are attended by a fundamental lack of the deeper forms of understanding of other peoples. With its emphasis on speed, the new technology encourages a superficiality of information at the expense of thought. Carey suggested that our infatuation with, and reliance upon, newer technology hinders our ability to grasp an argument, listen to foreign accents, or interpret complex cultures which are not our own. Moreover, Carey suggested that whereas on first view this worldwide telecommunications system should be a tool for international stability, in fact it expands the scale and consequences of our failures to communicate effectively with and to understand each other. He warned that if our skills of learning, understanding, and interpreting are not conserved, we may be left with a high-speed system in an exceedingly unstable world (Carey 1983, 48).

CORPORATE INTERESTS VERSUS PUBLIC INTEREST

In 1958 Murrow questioned whether the broadcast industry was accepting what he thought should be the greater social responsibilities of the field. He chided broadcast news divisions for their lack of courageous programming and their reluctance to tackle the issues of the day. In making this criticism Murrow was fully aware of the vulnerability of commercial broadcasting to financial pressures from advertisers and political pressures from Washington. Programmers often excused their poor decisions by claiming that they did not have the traditions built up by experience that the older media had; but, Murrow warned, "If they but knew it, they are building those traditions, creating those precedents every day. Each time they yield to a voice from Washington or any political pressure, each time they eliminate something that might offend some section of the community, they are creating their own body of precedent and tradition" (Bliss 1967, 356–57). As an example, the press was reluctant to resist political pressure when Secretary of State John Foster Dulles banned, by personal decree, any travel by American journalists to Communist China. Television networks entered only a mild protest and then promptly forgot the incident. Murrow, on the other hand, asked how the networks could serve the public interest under circumstances which left viewers relatively ignorant of cataclysmic changes occurring in a nation of six hundred million people. Such incidents allow the "precedent and tradition" of broadcasting to be shaped by political pressure and, according to Murrow, this is in the best interests of neither the public nor the medium itself.

Perhaps an even more pervasive influence on programming is economic. According to Edwin Diamond (1978, 143), in practice too many broadcasters worry about broadcasting anything that might interfere with the ringing of the cash registers. That this worry extends to news coverage is clear from Edward Jay Epstein's *News from Nowhere* (1973, 130), which points out that network news programs are governed to a great degree by the systematic application of economic principles. Since television networks make their money largely by selling advertising slots in their programs, they must try to "recruit" the largest audience they can for the advertisers' products. This circumstance tends not only to dictate the time at which the news is broadcast, but it also tends to affect the content of news reports; news documentaries, for example, will generally address noncontroversial, inoffensive topics in an attempt to maintain their audience. The program's success or failure in so doing will affect the network's income from advertisers and this will, in turn, dictate the amount of money and the resources which can be used in news gathering. In effect, these factors will determine the places from which news can be gathered, the subjects which can be covered, and the amount of time which can be spent in their treatment.

As our panelists note, the emphasis on being "first," scoop reporting, is one consequence of the struggle to maintain or increase audience figures for news programs. As a very real ethical issue, our panelists discuss the projection of winners through the increasing use of computer analyses of voting patterns in network coverage of presidential elections. In the 1980 and 1984 elections, newscasters in New York were able to make solid projections about the results even before the polling booths were closed in the western states. It was still late afternoon, Pacific time, and millions had yet to cast their votes. Panelist Wershba suggests that announcing to people on the West Coast that the president has been elected before they have voted destroys the essence of the democratic process. Other panelists concur, and yet all are doubtful whether any one network would take the lead and stop making such predictions since the risks of losing both audience and sponsorship are too great.

To counteract the influence of market pressures on program quality, Murrow proposed that each of the twenty or thirty largest corporations which dominate broadcasting give up one or two of their regularly scheduled programs each year and turn the time over to the networks as a commercial tithe for sponsoring programs on significant issues. Murrow believed that some such measure was necessary and that broadcasters should be responsible and sponsor a variety of programs, since "the premise upon which our pluralistic society rests, as I understand it, is that if the people are given sufficient undiluted information, they will then somehow, even after long, sober second thoughts, reach the right decision" (Bliss 1967, 362).

Murrow's sense of obligation to "the people" coincided with the mandate given television by the Federal Communications Act—that it serve the public interest, convenience, and necessity. Yet today, network apologists argue that television's attempts at public-interest broadcasting are fruitless because American audiences are not interested in such programming and are not mature or informed enough to handle complex information. Such assumptions about its audience led CBS to refuse to broadcast the Senate Vietnam hearings, which raises the question as to whether the Army-McCarthy hearings, momentous as they were, would have been broadcast if they had taken place in 1966 instead of 1954. Murrow was never afraid to risk losing his audience by tackling controversial subjects such as radioactive fallout and the banning of nuclear tests, and his risk paid off; he noted that viewers listened to both sides with reason and restraint (Bliss 1967, 355–56). The key question today is whether television news programs and their sponsoring networks have continued those early standards or maintained their previous commitments to public service.

INFLUENCE OF REPORTERS AND ORGANIZATIONS ON NEWS

One of the most difficult problems for media observers to resolve is that of attributing primary responsibility for the content of the news and the form in which it is presented. Who or what really determines the news — individual journalists, the organizations that employ them, the economic and political forces at work in society, or the naked events themselves? Murrow, as a reporter, regarded the role of the individual journalist as the most important in the process and resented the attempts of news organizations to influence the content of broadcasts. This emphasis, and Murrow's highly developed awareness of the responsibilities this placed on the reporter, led him to advocate a particular style of delivery. As he advised his European staff during World War II (Kendrick 1969, 246):

Never sound excited. Imagine yourself at a dinner table back in the United States, with the local editor, a banker, and a professor, talking over the coffee. You try to tell what it was like, while the maid's boyfriend, a truck driver, listens from the kitchen. Talk to be understood by the truck driver while not insulting the professor's intelligence.

Murrow's style set the standard by which other broadcasters were judged — "temperate yet crisp, dignified yet informal, understated and never condescending, and always probing behind the news."

Our panelists, like Murrow, place primary importance on the individual journalist, whose task they liken to that of the historian — reporting what they have seen or observed or know to be true. Scholars, however, have tended to regard such an emphasis as too simple. Herbert Gans (1979, 281), for example, in his study of network and national news magazine journalists, concluded that no single determining factor can be isolated. He noted that even though journalists exercise considerable control, in that they can judge the suitability of their sources and decide the way in which they use them, the reporter's autonomy is limited by the fact that the available sources tend to reflect the most powerful institutions and individuals in our society. Moreover, journalists have to work under the socioeconomic pressures of media organizations and local and national political and economic forces. This, too, tends to ensure that the news almost inevitably reflects established interests.

The ideal of objectivity in news reporting is also dispelled in Gaye Tuchman's *Making News* (1978, 158–61), an analysis of news organizations and the ways in which they shaped the selection, content, and presentation of stories. Tuchman's study showed that the way large and complex news organizations and networks structured their work influenced the news world that reporters encountered. Such organizations divided the world into territories — geographical areas, topical areas, or special beats — and assigned reporters accordingly. These arbitrary structures and the relationships built up within them — among individual reporters and between them and their sources — tended to lead to "news" that favored and reinforced the interests of established power. Thus, according to Tuchman, news is not and cannot be "objective," nor is it subject to much influence by individual reporters.

A final observation is that made by Walter Lippmann (1922, 214–25), who wrote that news content is determined by the coverage of events themselves. Before information can become news events, these events "usually have to make themselves noticeable in an overt act of an unmistakable form." That is, news is not a mirror of social conditions but the report of an aspect that has obtruded itself.

The precise attribution of responsibility for news content is, then, clearly difficult to make and prompts such disagreement. As news organizations and their bureaucracies grow more complex and more powerful, it seems as if individual journalists lose control over their own reports and yet, as we shall see in the next section, there are exceptions who, like Murrow, transcend those factors that would constrain them.

NEWS VISIONARIES

Media critics often complain today about the "star syndrome," the misplaced emphasis on the reporter's appealing image rather than on the quality of the information presented. Some thirty years ago when television was young, Murrow was concerned about this emphasis. He once asked if it was not possible that an infectious smile; clear, sincere eyes; or an air of authority might attract huge television audiences, regardless of the depth and quality of the reporting (Murrow, 1949, 4). At the same time, Murrow thought that as television news reached maturity, it would require even better furnished minds, offering greater breadth of information than print or radio.

The irony is that Murrow himself had those traits that are associated with "star quality": sincere eyes, a resonant voice, and *Casablanca* mysteriousness. However, he was by no means all image; he was a man of integrity and exemplary professionalism, whose acuity and insight justly earned him the title of visionary.

Our panel, like other media scholars and professionals, attempts to define those qualities in a broadcaster that could justly be called visionary and discusses those modern broadcasters who might deserve the title. They all mention such professional qualities as courage, honesty, and, of course, good reporting skills. In addition, according to panelist Charles Kuralt, a news visionary must have a fierce desire to inform people about those matters which might not appear immediately important but which have significant implications for the future. To do so, the broadcaster must be able to synthesize diverse facts and incidents and so see beyond the details of daily affairs to the significant patterns which lie behind them. Above all, however, the visonary must have moral integrity and the courage to write and produce controversial programs as honestly and straightforwardly as possible. Panelist Joe Wershba illustrates Murrow's code: "All I can do is teach my son to tell the truth and to fear no man."

When our panelists discuss those broadcasters who might be said to be following in Murrow's footsteps, they mention various names—Eric Sevareid, Howard K. Smith, Charles Collingwood, Jim Lehrer, Ted Koppel—but they all agree on news analyst Bill Moyers. Like Murrow, Moyers brings a wide experience to bear on his assignments and in them he displays a comparable integrity, courage, and professional style. He graduated from the University of Texas and then attended Southwestern Baptist Seminary before beginning a political career on Lyndon Johnson's staff. Moyers left Washington to become publisher of *Newsday*, after which he continued his media career in both public and commercial television, most recently as a public affairs commentator with CBS.

His Texas roots and theological background have led people to label him a populist and crusader, and Moyers does have a genuine commitment to and interest in presenting socially significant programs. In his broadcasts, at various times he has addressed historical, philosophical, political, sociological, and literary problems with consistent insight and occasional brilliance. Moreover, he has provocatively examined such controversial topics as chemical waste problems, the CIA, and military actions in Central America. Our panelists agree that his dedication to broadcasting in the public interest and his fair, objective treatment of difficult topics have earned him, more than any other, the right to be considered heir to the Edward R. Murrow tradition.

PANEL PARTICIPANTS

WILLIAM SMALL (*moderator*) was president and chief operating officer of United Press International in 1983. Small joined UPI in 1982 after serving three years as president of NBC News and as an executive of CBS News for seventeen years. He was head of the CBS Washington Bureau during the Watergate years and later became senior vice-president of CBS News.

CHARLES KURALT is anchor of CBS's "Sunday Morning" news program. For the past sixteen years, he has been a roving correspondent with his "On The Road" features. Kuralt made his debut on CBS as a writer in 1948 when Murrow read Kuralt's award-winning Voice of Democracy essay on the CBS radio evening news.

JOSEPH WERSHBA has been a reporter and producer for CBS News for nearly four decades. Wershba joined CBS News as a writer in 1944. Through the years he has served as a news director, Washington correspondent, and key member of documentary production units from the earliest "See It Now" productions to the present "60 Minutes" series.

I want to begin by reflecting about how news programs have changed in recent decades . . .

— BILL SMALL

Bill Small: I want to begin by reflecting about how news programs have changed in recent decades, particularly in response to changing technology; since Joe Wershba is the only one of us truly prepared for this session, we will start with him.

I have always been against computers in national elections.

— JOE WERSHBA

Joe Wershba: I am against the new technology. For instance, I have always been against computers in national elections. It is terrible for somebody in New York at eight o'clock on election night to announce to the people on the West Coast that the new president of the United States has already been elected. It destroys the essence of the democratic process that everyone has to feel that his vote counts, that he is in the process of electing his people. Each of you know that when President Carter conceded long before polls had closed on the West Coast, there were probably many people who questioned the need to go out and vote. It affected the local people too. In the old days there was an excitement to an election. In 1948 everybody was sent home at about five o'clock on election night morning. What was proved to me that night was that when you do not get a return by midnight, forget it, you are not going to get it until the next morning.

Bill Small: Let me offend this West Coast audience by taking issue with, on behalf of Bill Leonard and myself, Joe's contention about vote projection. It is an emotional issue in many places, in most political camps, and certainly in the western states. There are some things that one ought to recognize. Vote projection can only be done properly, successfully, in a landslide election, as indeed the Reagan election is the most dramatic example. It was called, if I remember correctly, at 5:20 PST, 8:20 EST, by NBC in 1980. It cannot be done in a close election, not if you are responsible. It was not done in the Kennedy/Nixon election, but there were early calls when Lyndon Johnson beat Barry Goldwater, for example.

. . . it is very hard to keep events, such as an election, secret for hours and hours.
—CHARLES KURALT

Charles Kuralt: It occurs to me to say that it is very hard to keep events, such as an election, secret for hours and hours. If it is clear to us at CBS or to any reporter that a new president has been elected, it goes against the grain to try to suppress this news from the American people. Maybe uniform poll closing time is the answer. That strikes me as a reasonable answer. But for an event to have occurred and for us to keep it secret even in the name of helping along the voting process on the West Coast strikes me as a perfectly terrible idea.

Joe Wershba: One could recommend that legislation be passed that the West Coast closes earlier, but in that case the East Coast stays open later—or else have twenty-four-hour voting. Every one of these suggestions has problems and that is why someone once quoted Ed as receiving a letter saying, I hate you Mr. Murrow because you never answer questions, you just ask me questions. The fact of the matter is that almost every suggested panacea has problems and I feel as Charles does that the worst thing we can do is suppress news. There are no really simple answers, nor is there adequate scientific evidence about the impact, even here in the West where it is such an emotional issue.

Another issue concerning news is the question of what do you do with all this technology. All the technology in the world, satellites, the nano seconds, and the pico seconds (which is a trillionth of a second), all conduct to give us the latest information and education. Well, what do you do with it? This is one of the *New York Post*'s greatest headlines.

Anybody in the business would be proud of this headline: "Headless Body in Topless Bar." There is no way you can forget that headline. It almost sings. It happens every day. Now that is one use of technology.

Another use of technology can be found in a very serious new newspaper, which I think is going to do very well, *USA Today*. It is printed all over the United States. I do not know how they do it but they turn out a beautiful newspaper and if I were running a newspaper, this would be my wire service. There is so much information on every page that I would take the story, give it a three column head, and bring it back to old style presentation. *USA Today* may be doing what they know the public now expects in a new age of technology; this may be the wave of the future. In other words, all the technology in the world is not going to do much if you do not know what to do with it.

Charles Kuralt: To tell you the truth, I do not think the technology has had so much of an effect. To be sure, in the old days we shot our film with black and white cameras and to be sure, the processing of it was slow. We would charter a plane in order to get it to a big city in order to fly it to New York in order that you could see it tomorrow. Except for speed, I cannot think offhand of any way in which the technology has affected the content of the news at all. I am not opposed to the new technology; it is a little handier for us to be able to shoot stories on video tape. "60 Minutes" still does its stories on film. Who in this audience cares whether they are done on tape or on film? It seems not to matter very much, it is the content of the book, the thoughts and the words and the pictures, finally, that are important. It is the people who do the work and not the technology that matter. The technology has just made it a little easier from my point of view.

Bill Small: If there is one thing that has run all through this symposium, it is the importance of integrity in reporting, and technology has nothing to do with that unless you let it corrupt you. Technology has had immense impact. I feel I am bookended by two young fogies here, but the fact of the matter is that now we have the opportunity to get material from distant points almost instantly or within a matter of minutes or just a few hours. And that does have impact on the question of journalism in the twentieth century.

If you go back to the days when there was neither radio nor television, newspapers were developing ways to distribute the news faster and faster. Then along came radio and television, and now satellite technology. We have sped up the pace of human life, and things that used to give us ample opportunities to dwell upon it, look on the dark side of it, or not know about it, no longer take days to reach us and change our opinions but sometimes take merely minutes or hours.

It is a mixed blessing. Fred Friendly always uses the phrase that what you don't know can kill you. Overall, it is much better that we know about things faster rather than slower and that is what the new technology has done for us. Management's point of view is that it has done great injury to the expense of newsgathering, most particularly in television. Yes, we can get a portable ground station in the middle of Africa, and cameras, and a charter, and get it on the air within a matter of hours, but the cost becomes overwhelming. When you accumulate the many times you do that during the course of any given year, the cost goes sky high. That is one of the troublesome effects of the new technology.

We talk about satellites and other things, but the fact is the question of advanced technology is not just for journalists but for historians and academics of all kinds; the fact is that the computer age can save you literally thousands of man-hours in doing research.

Charles Kuralt: There is a question in the program here which asks, if there are practicing news visionaries today, who are they? Visionaries may be too strong a word, but there are some imaginative people doing good work in television news today of a sort that has not been much done before. I am thinking of Jim Lehrer and Robin McNeil on their program in the early evening; of what Ted Koppel is doing, an extremely valuable program in the late evening. Probably Don Hewitt, the producer of "60 Minutes," qualifies as a visionary if anybody does, for having the imagination and the patience to press on with "60 Minutes" at a time when it was bouncing around the CBS network schedule and thought of as just another in a long string of ratings failures for news programs. It was later to become a profit center for CBS and perhaps the best one of all programs of any sort.

I would like to nominate Bill Moyers. If anybody is a visionary, I suppose he is. I think Ed would be proud of Moyers for carrying on in somewhat the Murrow style. That is, he is always fighting with the bosses and irritating them with memos and even worse with interviews of the press in which he says that television is not fulfilling its responsibilities. He brings to journalism something I surely have not had, most of us have not, a kind of evangelical fervor perhaps based on his earlier line of work as a Baptist preacher. But it is certainly based on a fierce wish to inform people about all sorts of important matters.

If you think back, you did not know Ed Murrow was a visionary until after he was gone. It was clear that he was the best reporter doing news on the air every day but he did it as we did, he just did it better. It is only now in retrospect that we can see that he does qualify. Yet it is hard to know who in the present crop of people on the air deserves that appellation.

Dan Rather was one of the best Washington reporters who has ever been on the air. I never understood how one could excel at the White House where, after all, the news is parceled out by the White House press offices. When I once had a chance to go to the White House, I turned it down. I could not imagine having any fun at that job but Dan Rather, when he had that job, had fun at it and did a very good job of informing the people. He was a novice yet contentious reporter. When you hear talk about merely pretty faces, nobody could really mean the admittedly very handsome face of Dan Rather. There is a good mind behind that handsome face. The same thing is true of Connie Chung, who was a very good street reporter in her time before she became a highly paid anchorwoman. It is hard to resent the big salaries of people like that.

At the local station level, there are a lot of young anchorpeople who do not have very much news experience, who are very good looking, very good performers but have no knowledge of nor any interest in their communities. They just sit down and say "good evening, here is the news," and would not in fact know a news story if it jumped up and mussed their coiffures. Their interest is in leaving San Antonio and going on to Cleveland, a little bigger market. That has been a great handicap to maturity in local news departments.

Bill Small: Since producers are paid so ungenerously comparatively, perhaps Joe you would like to add a footnote to that.

Joe Wershba: I have had very strong feelings about this over the years. The minute anybody in this business got paid more than an ordinary plumber or carpenter, we were in trouble. I am not worried about what anyone is making, I never cared about what they made. I never knew what Edward R. Murrow or Walter Cronkite made because they never made it a subject for public discussion or negotiation. It was not a matter of self-esteem with them. A lot of our troubles in the present period come from the fact that agents have been able to make their influence known on behalf of their correspondents, reporters, anchormen, and have begun to play a part in how newsrooms operate. When the so-called million dollar salaries began, we saw that in action. I find it a very dangerous thing. I do not think anybody should be in the newsroom who is not a member of the news department. I would have thrown them out. In the past, nobody was bigger than the organization itself. It does not make a difference who is in that spot, or else we are abdicating responsibility for running our own news department.

Barry Serafin has said he was glad to be working at ABC because he would pay them to do it even if they were not going to pay him. That was the spirit that really began this business, people love being in it. I meet a lot of young people; they come to see me and I die a million deaths when I see these talented young people because there is no place to get them in the news organization. I always have to tell them to go to a smaller operation, which is true, but they are good. They want to get in and they would like to do anything. Then there are others who are overwhelmed by what they think is the romance in it, the glamour, the money, and the rest of it, and that is not what telling the news is all about.

Just one last word on Murrow and what he represented. We have to keep telling ourselves the story because it is important for our business long after he is gone. Murrow gets brighter every year because he stands out like the burning star that never leaves the sky. Murrow's place in this whole news constellation was principally, preeminently, a place of moral leadership. He would not have been a writer; Eric Sevareid could write rings around him. He was not that much of a better reporter than Howard K. Smith; Howard K. Smith is an excellent reporter. I always preferred Charles Collingwood as an on-the-air man; I always thought he was the real inheritor of the Murrow tradition. Each one of these people had an edge in a certain respect over Ed, but when you put Ed Murrow together as a whole, there was nobody that came near him. They all wanted to be where he was.

He never wanted to go into television; he resisted it. The expression is that he was dragged screaming into the twentieth century, I am sure helped along by Fred Friendly. He did not like television because it was committee journalism at best, and at its worst too, but the minute that he and Friendly agreed they had to get into television, he was willing to make himself the goat. Up to that time, only Douglas Edwards was doing a regular news program, but the minute Murrow went on television, everybody else wanted to go into it. They wanted to be where he was. Why? Sure he was good looking, he had a nice voice, he knew all of his people, but he knew what the news business was all about, how to record it, and always the moral considerations that go with it.

That is why I say all the technology in the world is not going to mean anything. Ed, for instance, was anguished over the use of all the massive technology available to him in 1954 to put on the McCarthy program, which frankly, today, is just a good program until the last two minutes and then it is dynamite. What right, he asked, did he have to use all this equipment to go against one man or to make a point of view? He would have preferred not to have done that program, he would have preferred to have found another Radulovich or Annie Lee Moss. Maybe I am guessing at this because Murrow felt McCarthy had adequate resources to answer him, but most of all, he did the program because there was constant demagoguery and cowardice in this country at that time. It was necessary to stand up and say it lest we be held accountable into eternity for having failed to say it at that time. That is why he was my last hero; I have not had a hero since 1954. He was a patriot in the truest sense of the word.

Cicero had a rule about the role of the historian. The role of the historian, and just switch it over to the role of a journalist or reporter, is to report everything that he knows to be true, that he himself has seen or observed — not to report that which he knows to be false and not to leave out that which is significant and that he knows to be true. Now those are some good rules.

When Ed Murrow was under attack because of the McCarthy broadcast, I suppose that was the most livid I had ever seen him. His son Casey, who would have been nine or ten years old at the time, was in private school and had been brutalized by the kids in his school. They were calling his father a Communist. Ed could not deal with it. He said, "All I can do is teach my son to tell the truth and fear no man." That is a very good approach to news coverage. And it is Cicero's line.

There are a lot of other things you will find about libel and slander, of truth and coverage of news; they all go back thousands of years. Yet, all the technology in the world is not going to make the slightest bit of difference if you do not approach news and news gathering with a certain reverence and try not to make too many excuses for what we do or what we cannot do. It was Murrow who asked when name and conscience are able to talk to each other by telephone, will they have anything to say to each other? Technology works when you have the edge over the conversation.

Edward R. Murrow:
The Man and the Era

> A man is the product of his education, his work,
> his travel, his reading, all his experience.
>
> EDWARD R. MURROW
> *Upon receiving the Distinguished Alumnus Award,*
> *Washington State University, 1962*

DIANE SAWYER and many other journalists of today never met Edward R. Murrow, but they still look to him as a model who set standards for the profession. In her reflections on how journalists should prepare themselves for their different tasks, she suggests possible reasons why Murrow was a leader in his field. Edward R. Murrow was not an accident of history; he was a product of "the school of life," very much influenced by *all* of his experiences. That Murrow himself acknowledged this indebtedness is clear in the above quote from the speech he made in 1962, on his last visit to his college, Washington State University.

Most of us, when asked to define our "individuality," would do so in terms of our intelligence, aptitudes, temperament, and other qualities that we consider to be our own. But these qualities are never entirely given; they are to a degree shaped by our relationships to many different groups and experiences in a process that social scientists have come to call socialization. This process is continuous throughout a person's lifetime, as he or she learns the skills and orientations necessary to function in particular roles or in the larger society. Most obviously, our families teach us our basic attitudes, values, and sense of selfhood, and our schools offer a broader framework in which we learn to function in society. When we enter the work force we must learn appropriate work roles, attitudes, and orientations in order to succeed. Family, school, and work are not the only arenas of socialization

37

but they are the most important, and they played significant roles in the development of Edward R. Murrow.

Our objective, then, is to trace the influences and experiences that were central in Edward R. Murrow's development as an outstanding leader and visionary in mass media. We will not review his life in detail, since his biographer Alexander Kendrick does that very well. Instead, we want to place some aspects of Murrow's life in context and to add to the many points discussed by our panelists, who were his college friends and business associates.

FAMILY, EDUCATION, AND WORK

Edward R. Murrow was indeed the product of his family. During the war, Murrow would write his parents, "Whatever we have made of ourselves is due to the fundamental training we received at home" (Kendrick 1969, 87).

He was born Egbert R. Murrow in 1908 in Polecat Creek, North Carolina, where he lived until 1913 when his family moved to the Skagit Valley in Washington. Murrow's parents were Scotch-Irish with a strong southern heritage, and their influence had a marked effect in his development. His father, once called by a cousin "the workingest man" he had ever known, was "a man of resolve." The family, pillars of the Quaker community, spent many silent hours at Friends' meetings, reflecting upon the inward light. The home was an amalgam of sternness, forbearance, and responsibility, and Murrow never developed the capacity to relax completely and have fun. Murrow's brother Lacey once summed it up with, "They branded us with their own consciences." Murrow even referred to "the old Murrow conscience that's troubling me" (Kendrick 1969, 86, 251).

Murrow's mother had a tremendously strong influence upon her youngest son. Not only did he inherit the "Spenserian quality" of her southern voice, but she affected him in other ways, too. A former school teacher, she had an energetic, nervous disposition and was a strict disciplinarian. She and her family lived frugally and sparingly and she taught the boys a sense of respect for others—not just for their property, but for their opinions. She kept as an ideal the tight control of one's self, combined with a tolerance for others and a nonintrusion into their affairs. While she had a profound influence upon her sons' lives—all three boys had outstanding careers—she left their adult lives to their own discretion. While in London, Murrow wrote his parents, "I remember you once wanted me to be a preacher, but I had no faith, except in myself. But now I am preaching from a powerful pulpit. Often I am wrong, but I am trying to talk as I would have talked were I a preacher. One need not wear a reversed collar to be honest" (Kendrick 1969, 195).

Not only did the family have a profound influence upon Murrow, but so did life in the Northwest. After the family moved to the Skagit Valley in western Washington, the Murrow boys developed an intense love of the outdoors and an affinity with nature. While Egbert attended college, he financed himself by working summers in logging camps and managed to put enough aside to buy a small parcel of land on the installment plan. His brother Dewey said that "he always wanted ground he could possess" (Kendrick 1969, 86).

More than just a love of the out-of-doors, Murrow developed a toughness, an independent spirit, and a vitality through his work in the logging camps around the Olympic Peninsula. In these settings he became adept at arguing in the evenings around the campfires with the endless talking and listening. He was exposed, whether consciously or not, to the generally progressive, populist politics that set social patterns in the Pacific Northwest (Kendrick 1969, 99, 93; Jackson 1965, 8487).

Murrow's education was another component in his individual development. His early interest in books and school is shown by a photograph taken when Egbert was not yet old enough to attend. His brothers were about to set off for the first day of classes and the young Egbert was with them, clutching a book. He was a square little boy with a round face and a determined chin thrust downward. His biographer Kendrick (1969, 83) wrote: "This facial expression, later to become lean instead of round, remained with him all his life for special dire occasions, both on the television screen and off. Some would call it his doomsday look." Our panelist Jack Friel refers to that determined Murrow, a man on the side of truth and justice.

In high school all three Murrow brothers were extracurricular leaders, even though their classroom grades were not remarkable. In keeping with the times, Murrow played the ukulele, was on the baseball and basketball teams, and served both as class president and student body president. Naming him as the boy who had done the most for the school and citing his charm, his class predicted that he would be a "professor of social science at the University of Washington and that later, he would speak on social reform" (Kendrick 1969, 93, 95).

Our keynote speaker Diane Sawyer is correct when she later notes that Murrow did not come to Washington State University with a desire to be a journalist, but rather with a rambunctious and bright mind. In fact, he enrolled in business administration before changing to speech (Kendrick 1969, 100). Our panelists Paul Coie and Jack Friel tell us about life at this university and in Pullman, Washington, during the late 1920s.

Murrow changed a lot during his college years—he even changed his name from Egbert to Edward during his sophomore year and became "Ed" to most people. As you will hear from our panelists, he went, in a matter of several years, from class president to student body president to president of the National Student Federation in 1929.

In the classroom Murrow was mostly a "B" student, except in speech and military training. He was not as interested in the written word as he was in the spoken. He toiled through term papers and theses. Moreover, he was a poor speller and had atrocious handwriting. Yet he acted, debated, and orated and, as Paul Coie says, he looked resplendent in his ROTC uniform. By the time he graduated in 1930 with a Bachelor of Arts in Speech, he was also a member of two scholastic honorary societies—even though his highest mark was the unofficial "A-plus" awarded him for his personality by the Chinook yearbook (Kendrick 1969, 107).

Diane Sawyer and panelist Robert Sandberg refer to the influence of Murrow's college mentor, Ida Lou Anderson. She was a caring, sensitive teacher; Sandberg aptly calls her a remarkable fountain of flame and spirit. She had been Murrow's declamation coach, his dramatics advisor, and his speech professor. She turned Murrow from a natural debater and broadcaster into a serious, skilled, and polished one. Moreover, with her hunched body warped by infantile paralysis, she gave Murrow an example of courage that he never forgot (Kendrick 1969, 104).

Murrow's attitude toward his own work had a tremendous impact on who he was as a man. As our panel members point out, he was continuously successful. He never stopped growing, he never stopped learning. Murrow took his first job with the National Student Federation, filling a position which, as panelist Sharnick points out, Murrow had helped to create. Murrow, the ideal listener and commentator, would interview scholars such as Albert Einstein for both the National Student Federation and the Institute of International Education. Displaying his ability to seize upon and distill the thoughts of others while adding dimensions of his own, Murrow created forceful new syntheses and conclusions in these interviews. His trips to Europe both increased his ever-widening circle of acquaintances and furthered his persistent pursuit of education. In 1935, as director of Talks and Education for CBS, Murrow continued his work in international education. He later recalled that his experiences at this time, especially his conversations with refugee German scholars, had been "a sort of revolving seminar" (Kendrick 1969, 111, 112, 126).

Murrow had a tremendous capacity to drive himself. He kept long hours and complained with pride to his wife that the physical fatigue to which this led was a kind of accolade of self-satisfaction. Later, he would write, "I've driven myself terribly in the past few years to get where I am." He even wrote his wife Janet a forecast of his future when he said in 1934 that he "was working so hard that the doctors were 'threatening' him with a nervous breakdown" (Kendrick 1969, 120, 124).

Murrow's dependency upon his work as a definition of himself was a part of his very being which never changed. He had never known life without work. His mother's firm discipline and constant supervision was combined with her stated belief, "it was better to wear out than to rust out" (Kendrick 1969, 81–82).

THE RIGHT MAN IN THE RIGHT PLACE
IN THE RIGHT ERA

Even though his mother instilled in her young son a strong sense of courage, integrity, and other values that stood him well throughout his career, neither Murrow's family life nor his early years were extraordinary. It is doubtful that observers would have marked him out for the great career he eventually achieved. His family, education, and early work experiences clearly nurtured his talents and abilities and provided a solid foundation for his later achievements, but these things alone were not sufficient. According to David Halberstam (1979, 38), Ed Murrow was

The right man in the right place in the right era. An elegant man in an up to then inelegant profession; one of those rare legendary figures who was as good as his myth.

Because of Murrow's outstanding success with the National Student Federation and the Institute of International Education, he was hired by CBS as director of Talks and Education in 1935, just five years after he had received his Bachelor's degree. Shortly thereafter, in 1937, when an opening occurred, Murrow was named director of CBS's European Division, a behind-the-scenes programming job lining up European officials for broadcasts. In the process, Murrow became acquainted with many prominent figures, among them Winston Churchill. The international situation grew more ominous under the threat of Hitler's expansionism, and when war broke out, Murrow became an integral part of the broadcast world, despite his lack of journalistic experience. Halberstam (1979, 41) says it well: "Murrow overnight became a journalist. He was a natural for his role and he was part of a vast change; it was the dawning of a new and sometimes terrible modern age." Murrow witnessed some of the most dramatic and destructive events of human history, and he combined his talent for description and his baritone voice to launch his broadcast career at the start of World War II. He was indeed at the right place at the right time.

Unlike later wars in which the United States was involved, World War II could be seen as a heroic conflict; the survival of the center of western civilization was at stake. In time, Americans realized that their own survival was threatened, and Murrow consequently became a hero of a heroic war. His relationship to the war was clearly crucial to Murrow's success. As Halberstam (1979, 40) notes:

In normal times there would have been no way for Murrow to have been Murrow. . . . But World War II was special and he was special, the first great professional radio voice . . . a voice steeped in intelligence and civility and compassion and sensitivity. . . . This meant that when he came back to America he was a superstar with prestige and freedom and respect within his profession and within his company.

Murrow also was in the right place at the right time in the development of two communication technologies — radio and television. In reflections about Murrow's life, former CBS news editor Edward Bliss (1975, 18) states: "In the whole history of journalism, perhaps no other reporter has become famous quite so fast. This was due not only to the quality of Ed Murrow's reporting but also to the medium itself." He was referring in this case to radio, but years later the same was said about Murrow and television.

During World War II radio reached a mass audience unmatched by any other medium. Not only was it faster, but it was more personable than print, and it created vivid, dramatic pictures in the minds of millions. According to Bliss (1975, 18), "Murrow was transformed in the public mind, as by magic, from being one of many reporters covering the Battle of Britain to the reporter covering that battle."

With each new development in broadcasting, Murrow was there. When Hitler went into Austria, Murrow provided Americans with a European radio relay hookup. In 1948 he provided commentary for the first televised political convention. As the networks switched their emphasis from radio to television news, Murrow was directly involved. When Americans first saw television monitors showing simultaneously the Brooklyn Bridge and the Golden Gate Bridge provided by the first coast-to-coast coaxial cable and microwave relays, Murrow was there. Murrow had offered this comment on the debut of *See It Now*: "Good Evening. This is an old team trying to learn a new trade" (Kendrick 1969, 337). And learn it he did. Before he died, a new era of communication technology had begun; for example, the Telestar Satellite allowed an instantaneous transmission of live events across oceans and between continents. We can only speculate on the ways in which Edward R. Murrow would have capitalized on these developments had he lived.

Edward R. Murrow used changing broadcasting technology to his advantage. He had special qualities that enabled him to exploit the vast changes of the era. What was it about Murrow that was so special that even some eighteen years later, friends, broadcasters, and media scholars regard him in legendary terms and label him a visionary, a gallant fighter, a shooting star, a poet of mankind, and a philosopher-king? He had all-so-rare creative talents, and he persistently applied them to all of his endeavors. Many of our speakers, not only on this panel, but on others too, refer to the Murrow genius.

The special talents that characterized Murrow are shared by other creative people who make significant contributions to their respective fields. Bill Moyers (1982, 72) in his recent PBS series "Creativity" defined the core of creativity as innovation — the ability to go beyond existing patterns and rules. He and others agree that there are special qualities that motivate creative people to strive beyond the ordinary. Creative people are imaginative, innovative, and have the ability, according to Moyers, to look at the commonplace and find the strange. They also approach the world and their interests with enthusiasm or as Moyers called it, "a childlike wonder." Motivated in part by this enthusiasm, creative people have moments of great insight; they invent, they do something new, they forge through the frontiers of a field. These breakthroughs do not just happen—creative people make them happen. They have uncommon drive; they have dedication and persistence; and they have unusual self-discipline (Austin 1978, 112–18). Comments from our speakers reveal glimpses of Murrow's creative genius as he changed the course of broadcast journalism beyond the superficial, the trivial, and the obvious.

Perhaps James Reston (1965, A44) explained Murrow's genius best when he wrote that Murrow hated the commercial rat race of television networks and their frivolities and constantly fought for emphasis on the great issues of life. According to Reston:

He grew up in an age that rewarded good looks and the mastery of techniques and longed for the spirit of a simpler age. . . . He was a reporter of the old school and a performer of the new. In radio and television there is no written permanent record; only the memory of the listener remains. And the memory of Ed Murrow will remain for a long time among people who remember the terrible and wonderful days of the Battle of Britain.

PANEL PARTICIPANTS

DEAN MELL (*moderator*) was president of the Radio Television News Directors Association and has been news director at KHQ-AM/ FM TV, Spokane, since 1973. Prior to joining the station, Mell spent eleven years with NBC News in San Francisco and New York.

PAUL COIE is a member of the law firm of Perkins, Coie, Stone, Olsen, and Williams in Seattle, Washington. He is a fellow and past regent of the American College of Trial Lawyers and a past president of the Seattle-King County Bar Association. Coie was a classmate of Murrow and graduated with him from WSU in 1930.

JACK FRIEL spent thirty years as head basketball coach at WSU from 1928 to 1958. Following his retirement, Friel served for eight years as commissioner of the Big Sky Athletic Conference.

ROBERT SANDBERG is senior advisor to the Electric Power Research Institute in Menlo Park, California. He has served on the faculty of the University of Illinois, as an executive with the Red Cross, as an executive assistant to WSU President Wilson M. Compton, and as a public relations officer and vice-president of the Kaiser Corporation. Sandberg is also the author of three books on public speaking.

JOHN SHARNIK retired from CBS News in 1982 as senior executive producer of Prime-Time Documentaries. From 1975 to 1977 he served as CBS News vice-president and director, Public Affairs Broadcasts. Previously, he was an editor of the *New York Times* Sunday Department.

Murrow gave all of us who have followed in his path benchmarks for honest and courageous reporting.

— DEAN MELL

Dean Mell: I presume to represent the thousands of working broadcast reporters and news directors at this distinguished event. Radio Television News Directors Association (RTNDA) represents those broadcast journalists who collect, write, and report the news that most Americans rely upon for their awareness of what is happening in their world. For us, Edward R. Murrow represents the standard of excellence by which we measure our own work. RTNDA's highest award for news reporting is given annually in his name. Mr. Murrow himself was awarded RTNDA's most prestigious citation, the Paul White award, in 1964.

Someone was quoted as saying, "If radio only had pictures, there would be no need for television." Well, I am here to tell you when Edward R. Murrow spoke, radio did have pictures. The most powerful kind, the kind we see in the mind's eye. Viewing the horrors of Buchenwald as he accompanied the allied liberators into that horror filled camp, Murrow told his radio listeners that the "feeble survivors greet their rescuers with applause that sounds like the hand clapping of babies."

To broadcast journalists, Edward R. Murrow is the founder of what we call in-depth reporting. By example, Murrow showed the rest of us broadcast reporters that we could do more than recite bulletin board items. If Murrow could use broadcast tools and human skills to give an audience deeper insights and better understanding, then so might the rest of us. Murrow's work decisively moved broadcast journalism toward a goal that was defined by the Commission on Freedom of the Press. In the late forties, the commission report told journalists that they are most useful when they give a "truthful, comprehensive and intelligent account of the day's events in a context which gives them meaning. It is no longer enough to report fact truthfully," the commission said, "it is now necessary to report the truth about the facts." Edward R. Murrow did that routinely, before the commission published its report, with his legendary London broadcasts and of course later with the honored "See It Now" series. Murrow understood that it was not enough to report only what happened but also to report why it happened. Murrow gave all of us who have followed in his path benchmarks for honest and courageous reporting.

He must have changed rooms . . . every week or so, because in the ensuing years I have met more men who claimed they roomed with Ed.

—PAUL COIE

Paul Coie: The thoughts I would like to share with you today are what this university was like about fifty years ago when Ed was a classmate of mine. The enrollment in 1926 was about 3,000 students. The town of Pullman had about 3,000 people. The size created a sense of familiarity and an environment that I would characterize as gentle.

Living costs were cheap. The 1929–1930 catalog indicates that the average cost of room and board in the sororities and fraternities was thirty-five to forty dollars a month. The college library in 1929 had only 180,000 bound volumes.

Pullman was not filled with exciting night life but there was a public dance hall we called the Green Lantern where dances were held from time to time. Cars were virtually unknown and only known by a few affluent students. Athletics had strong student support on campus, as you might expect. However, in 1930 Washington State College won the Rose Bowl. This was the second time, the first being 1910.

The environment and flavor of the town and college had a strict moral tone. The dean of women crawled into her office one night to observe fraternity boys cheering unclad girls who failed to pull down the shades when they were dressing. In her reprimand, the dean told the girls that the human body is not beautiful, only babies are.

This is the background and now I will turn to Ed. He was extremely handsome. He was resplendent in his ROTC officer uniform, a subject he took seriously, and this was proved by his being a cadet colonel. He was interested in dramatics and had leads in such plays as *The Youngest*, *Greg's Life*, *The Evening*, and Eugene O'Neil's *Beyond the Horizon*.

He must have changed rooms in Kappa Sigma house, of which he was president, every week or so, because in the ensuing years I have met more men who claimed they roomed with Ed.

Ed was also interested in campus politics. He was junior class president and senior year president of the student body. This led to his election as president of the National Student Federation, a relatively unknown organization. Ed left for New York in the depth of the depression, 1930, walked up and down Madison and debated enough men to create a fund that allowed him to rent a room, pay himself a salary of twenty-five dollars a week, and travel to the campuses throughout the United States.

I was admiringly aware that Ed always came out on the side of truth and justice, that his sympathies were always on the side of the underprivileged in this country.

— JACK FRIEL

Jack Friel: My first contact with Ed was on the basketball court when I returned to Washington State College in 1928. Ed was a junior then and I became acquainted with him. I was much more closely associated with his brother, Lacey, with whom I lived my last two years in college. Lacey later became highway director for the state of Washington and was quite an operator.

During the war, I would turn on the radio nightly and listen for Ed's introduction which became so famous, "This . . . is London." We appreciated his fine descriptions of the bombing of London, bomber runs over Germany, and the rest of his reporting on the war. I was most interested in Ed's career when he was promoted by CBS along with Fred Friendly of the Public Service broadcast, and his shows, "See It Now," "CBS Reports," and other documentaries. I knew something of the difficulties attendant to such broadcasts. At that time, those programs were not very attractive from the standpoint of the networks. They engendered a lot of criticism and opposition among those they exposed. For instance, in the broadcast on Joe McCarthy, I was surely glad to see those broadcasts contribute to the political down slide of McCarthy, but I know that they engendered severe criticism from the political extreme right in this country. "A Harvest of Shame," in which the deplorable conditions among the migrant workers in this country were exposed, also attracted a great deal of criticism from powerful agricultural forces in this country.

Later, I read Friendly's book, *Due to Circumstances Beyond Our Control,* and realized the tremendous fight Friendly and Murrow faced in the interest of public service and public service telecasts. To me, the courage and determination, dedication, as shown in the development of those programs, epitomized the best qualities of Edward R. Murrow, the man. I was admiringly aware that Ed always came out on the side of truth and justice, that his sympathies were always on the side of the underprivileged in this country.

I know that anyone who knew
Ida Lou Anderson would recognize
in Ed Murrow her hallmarks.
—ROBERT SANDBERG

Robert Sandberg: There is an old trite statement which says that great teachers make great universities. Not often do they also add that great teachers often make great people. Every one of us probably has had one teacher who was special in his life, who made a lasting impression, who helped develop motivation or set the tone on which a career is built. I know that anyone who knew Ida Lou Anderson would recognize in Ed Murrow her hallmarks.

Ida Lou Anderson was a remarkable woman. She would have been remarkable even if she had been physically normal, but she was cruelly warped, twisted, and hunched by infantile paralysis. However, to her students, she was a fountain of flame and spirit and caring. She was Ed Murrow's favorite teacher and he was Ida Lou's favorite student. She taught a course called simply, "Interpretation." There were three or four progressive courses in it, one for beginners, for intermediates, and one for advanced students. Ed Murrow took all of them. Miss Anderson did not lecture, she did not use textbooks, there were no formal examinations. She took her students as they came: bashful, brawny, sensitive, arrogant, hearty, serious, and a little lethargic as students often are. Each was treated as an individual and graded on personal progress from their entering level. Her goal was to help each student find something in literature that would stir an inner emotion or create a shimmer of light, however dim, through reading aloud. Ida Lou Anderson assigned passages of prose and poetry for study, to practice, to read aloud to the class. She sat always in a corner chair in the back of the room and after each meeting she conducted a very provocative, searching, wide-ranging critique. Her purpose was to motivate the students to find all the meaning in the given passage: the authors intent, in thought, in mood, in sound, in beauty. Then the student was to project that to the class. For some, the experience was unfamiliar and humbling. Many people thought it was a snap course.

For serious students like Edward R. Murrow, there were private sessions with Ida Lou, discussions really, and reading aloud together. Ida Lou believed as John Ruskin, that you might read all the books in the British museum if you could live long enough and still remain an utterly illiterate, uneducated person, but if you read ten pages of a good book, letter by letter, that is to say with real accuracy and meaning, you are forever more in some measure an educated person. I am sure that Murrow acquired his talent for extracting full meaning from words through association with this dedicated teacher.

Ed Murrow spent much time with Ida Lou Anderson. He often escorted her to plays and concerts here in Bryan Hall. As with others, their association continued after graduation. They corresponded for years. Ida Lou Anderson is credited with helping Ed Murrow develop the little pause between "this" and "is London" that became his famous trademark during the battle for Britain and beyond. He urged her to cable him in London with comments and statements that he could use in his broadcast back to the states. She declined because that would have been out of character for her. She was not interested in participation; her strength was in helping others develop their skills and even with her beloved student, Ed Murrow, she wouldn't change.

In a personal letter Miss Anderson once wrote to me, "the combination of strength and tenderness," is what she likes most in a man. "A man who had a hold of his work, his philosophy; the tolerant acceptance of people including himself. A man with a stoic nature, toughened and sweetened by experience," and then referring specifically to Murrow, she wrote, "his observations are usually ones of actual experience which carry with them implications of a broader nature. One gets weary of hearing how many planes were brought down." "I like something," she says, "along with that which makes me know a man in Europe is really a man in Europe." When Ida Lou died in September of 1941, Ed wrote a brief statement for her memorial. He said, "a tribute to her should employ the eloquence of the ancients and it should be read aloud." She was a polar skeptic, he said, "who believed nothing and had reverence for all. She demanded not excellence so much as integrity. She could recognize not only ability but humility and she was inclined to place more value on the latter." In those few lines it seems to me that Edward R. Murrow not only paid tribute to his teacher but inadvertently described himself.

His personal values were his professional standards.
— JOHN SHARNIK

John Sharnik: There is an ancient belief that great men radiate a kind of karma or a physical aura that blesses and ennobles everyone in its presence.

The group of extraordinarily bright and talented men whom Ed Murrow hired to work for him at CBS News seemed to share in this aura. It has proven to be extraordinarily durable. They were originally known as Murrow's spearhead boys. It has been eighteen years since he died and they are still known as Murrow's boys. I am not one of the blessed group. I am not here as one of Murrow's boys and I am not here as one of his many Kappa Sig brothers. I can claim no such blood tie but I think I know what Ed would have said if he had been here today.

He most likely would have begun by expressing regret that such a brilliant occasion as this was being wasted on a television commentator. That was how he sometimes referred to himself in a spirit of self-deprecation, a mere television commentator. One of a species that is best known for a tendency to think with their tonsils and who do not know what is on their mind until they have said it. That kind of gentle self-mockery was one important facet of the Murrow style. He distrusted his own celebrity and he seemed to take a special pleasure in letters from viewers and listeners which put him down. One that he quoted a lot as his favorite was from a woman who wrote, "I've been waiting for years and you still never tell me the answer to anything. Not only that but you usually wind up asking me questions."

Now, in the privacy of his own thoughts, of course, Ed Murrow would never have described himself as a commentator any more than he would have called himself an anchorman. If he had written an autobiography, it would have been the story primarily of his experiences as a reporter. That was his primary identity. When he wanted to avoid saying I, the word he used was reporter.

Murrow, as anyone who has worked with him in our business will tell you, was an extraordinarily private individual. He was not given to expressions of personal emotion although he had a remarkable ability to invest external events with deep emotional content. A *Time* magazine writer once observed that "Murrow made you feel about the possible defeat of Britain in World War II as personally as you would about the death of a child." But in his personal relations he was a man of great reserve. He once told an interviewer who also happened to consider himself a good friend that "I've never had any intimate friends, only colleagues and acquaintances." This may be about as close to a public self-revelation as Murrow ever came.

The closest thing to an autobiography that he ever managed to write is a sketch that he batted out for the CBS press department late in 1953, and it is very sketchy. Here, for example, is what he wrote about his boyhood on the Olympic peninsula, the timber country in the western part of this state, where his family moved from North Carolina when he was about six. Ed wrote, "Although we lived on tidewater, I never learned to swim, because there was always work to be done." He also once said that, "there was never a time I didn't have to work, I never developed a capacity for fun." Beginning at age fourteen he goes on, "spent summers in logging camp, working as a whistle pump woodcutter and later donkey engine fireman. Learned something about the lumber industry and acquired an extensive vocabulary of profanity." He rarely used it. I have found some of his old colleagues that have had to rack their brains to verify a certain alleged "goddamn" for me.

About his career at this institution Murrow wrote, "Worked my way through college washing dishes and shifting scenery in the theatre. Worked one winter in sorority house for a free bed in the basement. Used to listen to sorority sisters on floor above engaging in late night truth parties. Very instructive. Took courses ranging from animal husbandry to historic costuming. Was very active in extracurricular affairs, debating, dramatics. Elected class president junior year. Cadet colonel of ROTC, president of student counsel and president of Pacific Student Federation." He was, in other words, a success before he ever left this campus and he simply went on from there.

His job as president of the National Student Federation led directly to one that would have been considered extraordinary even for someone five or ten years older than Ed. He was underaged for it and, indeed, he lied about his age in getting the job as assistant director of the Institute of International Education. The institute was a foundation that brought refugee scholars over here from Europe when Nazism was already starting to rise and helped to place them on American campuses. Ed later described that as, "the most gratifying and instructive experience of my life." He was not excluding broadcasting when he said it gave him a sense of humanitarian achievement. It brought him in contact with the finest minds one could hope to associate with in any field.

He was only twenty-seven when he was recommended to the Columbia Broadcasting System for the job of executive in charge of what we would now call cultural broadcasts. He was just twenty-nine when CBS sent him to Europe as, in effect, executive in charge of producing special events broadcasts, coronations, festivals, concerts, and the like. He was sensitive to the events and issues of the time. The gathering shadow of war in Europe launched the network's regular coverage of international news and coincidently, almost serendipitously, diverted Murrow from a career in management to a career as a journalist, the preeminent foreign correspondent of his generation. He worked out of London for nine years, then came home after the war to run CBS News, which was by now emerging as one of the most powerful news-gathering organizations in the world, no little thanks to Murrow. A colleague surveying this remarkable record of triumphs starting with his days right here at Pullman, shook his head in sympathy and said, "Poor Ed. All his life plagued with success."

By his own account he did not make a success of the top job. He stayed with the position of vice-president of CBS News for two years and inevitably went back to his love. Ed went back to reporting with his daily news commentary on radio, with the weekly series "See It Now" in which he and Fred Friendly invented the television documentary, with his celebrity interview series "Person to Person," which in terms of popularity was the "60 Minutes" of its day and finally, briefly, with a then-new documentary series called

"CBS Reports." For one solid decade, the decade of the fifties, Ed Murrow was the preeminent broadcaster, the preeminent journalist, the Walter Cronkite, Dan Rather, Mike Wallace, all rolled into one, of his day. He was, you might say, the prototype of that current phenomenon, the media superstar. The chairman of CBS, Bill Paley, was asked once at a stockholders meeting why Murrow was being paid more than the chairman of the board and Paley simply replied, "because he's more valuable."

Murrow's departure from broadcasting in 1961 to serve in the Kennedy administration as director of the United States Information Agency is explained probably as an act of final disillusionment with the medium he had been publicly and increasingly criticizing. Like American corporate business, in general, broadcasting became increasingly concerned with growth, diversification, and the bottom line, meaning instant profits. In the broadcasting business in particular, this meant mass audience, high ratings, top programming, all of which are obvious facts of life and recent history that we have all experienced and observed. There is possibly an additional, more illusive explanation of Murrow's estrangement from television, from broadcasting. Television is an extraordinarily consuming business, it is our beloved monster and the documentary, Ed Murrow's specialty, is a particularly consuming form. You immerse yourself in it for just so long that sometimes it is hard to get back to the surface. Murrow, a particularly intense and conscientious man, an intense and conscientious worker, had fed himself to the monster, piece by piece, week by week, and perhaps he felt there was just nothing left.

As you consider this career, this life, there is one particular quality about it, about these facts that emerge as you dig through the scripts, the speeches, the letters, and other private papers that Murrow left for other reporters. There is a quality that strikes you and that quality is consistency, the life consistent with the work, the reporter consistent with the man. His personal values were his professional standards. Murrow, the extremely private individual, as I mentioned earlier, was also a reporter with almost religious respect for other people's privacy and individuality. Critics felt he leaned over backwards.

His interviews on "Person To Person" were unquestionably soft. "Person To Person," Murrow explained, "is a program in which I through our cameras appear as an invited guest in other people's homes. I can hardly be expected to ring the doorbell, step inside and proceed to ask my host and hostess embarrassing questions." But even in other circumstances, Murrow was not a tough interviewer, which is not to say he was not a tough reporter. In this business he said, "Over the years you collect enemies because you occasionally must hurt people." He also said, apropos of the essential adversary role of the press towards the government, "I subscribe to vice-president Barclay's maxim that a political reporter has to be against everybody, some."

It isn't to say also that Murrow was without guile or craft as a journalist. Here is what he once said about how to interview a political or military leader for television. He did not say this to an American audience, interestingly. "The indispensable asset," he said, "is an ability to smile and wait. If you put a direct question, the interviewee will answer it in the same way he has probably answered that same question dozens of times before. He thinks he is giving you the definitive answer. You manage a slightly puzzled, uncomprehending expression. He thinks to himself, and I've known one or two to say it aloud, you stupid oaf, if you didn't understand that then I'll proceed to put it into language that even you can understand, and proceeds to do so. In the course of editing, you throw out the first answer and use the second one." And he concluded, "that's about all or maybe more than I know about conducting an interview for television."

But Murrow was not the kind of interviewer whose technique was to get under a person's skin. He preferred to get inside it. He had that capacity that distinguishes the best practitioners of journalism like Eric Sevareid and Bill Moyers, the capacity to treat his enemies like human beings, the capacity to treat people that he disagreed with respectably, decently. Practically everything Murrow did was infused with a moral tone, all his reporting, all his commentary. History was full of lessons, events all around us were freighted with warnings and examples. He moralized about them, but he did this without being judgmental. He did not place himself as a reporter above the person he was reporting about or above the audience he was reporting to.

For all that moralizing, he was remarkably free of that sanctimonious quality that characterizes so much of journalism in the post-Vietnam, post-Watergate generation. He did not seem to feel holier than thou, whether thou were an isolationist senator, an American legionnaire, or even a lowly president of the United States. Murrow seemed to operate on the interesting assumption that a journalist had no right to be surprised if legislators, generals, doctors, or judges turned out to be no wiser, no more honest, no less venal, or no less cynical than journalists. And now at a time when reporters often go forth on missions not so much of enlightenment as of combat, when an interview is sometimes less an engagement of minds than a test of machismo, and when a story is sometimes considered not so much in terms of what light it may cast on the human condition as what opportunities it offers to make a score against some authority figure, at a time when the public sometimes views the media less as its champion than as an antagonist, when the public and sometimes the courts seem to suspect that the First Amendment is being used not so much as a shield but as a privileged sanctuary for journalistic gorillas, at a time like this I think it is useful and gratifying to contemplate the work of a reporter named Edward R. Murrow and to celebrate the man.

The Dilemmas of War Coverage: From the London Blitz to the Beirut Battles

The first casualty when war comes is truth.

SENATOR HIRAM JOHNSON, *1917*

PHILLIP KNIGHTLEY argued in *The First Casualty* that during wartime, governments extinguish truth through propaganda and censorship. Supposedly, these controls over information and knowledge are implemented in support of war efforts on the assumption that full reporting of wartime activities might be dangerous to the security of the nation. Panel member Clete Roberts labels this type of government control of information security censorship. However, there is another type of government control of information, which he terms policy censorship, involving the suppression of information that might embarrass military leaders or political figures. While journalists usually submit voluntarily to security censorship during national crises, Roberts asserts that no responsible correspondent willingly submits to policy censorship.

Governments exert various types and degrees of information control during different types of wars. The war correspondent panelists, whose assignments have ranged from the declared World War II to more recent limited Middle Eastern skirmishes, have firsthand knowledge of the dilemmas of war coverage. They, like Edward R. Murrow, have faced the competing and conflicting issues and principles in the interactions between media and government in times of crises.

War is news, probably the most important national and international news. Some war news, however, could conceivably subvert a country's war

53

effort. Today, reporters are anxious to report war news but at the same time they are loathe to become overt collaborators of either their own or the opponent's government. In most cases, they just want to tell the story. War coverage offers a particularly sensitive dilemma to the American journalist because of the basic values and rights that are at the heart of American society.

The First Amendment guarantees freedom of speech and of the press, both of which are basic to the development and maintenance of an informed electorate in a democratic society. And yet in wartime, situations may arise in which these freedoms may be legitimately curtailed. On these occasions the journalist has to resolve the conflicting demands of his responsibility as a citizen to his government's prosecution of the war and his responsibility as a journalist to tell his story. Edward R. Murrow had to face this dilemma in his reporting of action during the Battle of Britain. Thus the delicate relationship between the American media and government during wartime illustrates how Murrow and other correspondents have balanced these conflicting pressures.

THE PRESS IN A DEMOCRACY

While there have been fierce battles over free expression during this country's last 200 years, it is primarily during wartime or under the threat of war that the American courts have excepted the First Amendment clause of "Congress shall make no law . . . abridging the freedom of speech or of the press. . . ." First Amendment scholar Thomas I. Emerson wrote that curtailment of free expression in the name of "national security" can readily undermine the entire system. Once freedom of expression is subordinated to the vague demands of national security, there is no end to the sham of subsequent restrictive measures. Emerson (1972, 170) suggested that the danger was even larger as "past experience suggests that the withholding of information from the public in periods of crisis creates more public anxieties and hostilities that are directed against the government which in turn provoke every repressive measure."

Alexander Meiklejohn (1948, 36) went further than Emerson. He wrote that the First Amendment is and must be absolute for all public affairs. Meiklejohn noted the irony inherent in the fact that while the populace may be prohibited from speaking, as in wartime, Congress is protected from such abridging interference. Meiklejohn asked might not congressional debates also bring about a serious and an immediate threat to the general welfare. He said, "On the floor of both houses, national policies have been criticized with an effectiveness that words could never achieve." Meiklejohn noted that in an emergency, there could be no assurance that partisan ideas would be given a fair and intelligent hearing.

The First Amendment protects free expression and infers the public's "right to know"; yet this too is not absolute. John C. Merrill (1973, 461) noted that the right-to-know expression sounds much more democratic than the simple term "freedom of the press" and shifts the theoretical emphasis from a private and restricted institution, the mass media, to the much broader base of the American citizenry. Court decisions have affirmed that people can read or see what they want in the privacy of their homes. Federal open-meeting laws and the Freedom of Information Act have allowed both citizenry and media greater access to government information than ever before. However, legal limits have been established on the flow of information during periods of national threat. (For a fuller discussion see Baldasty and Simpson 1981, 394.)

Panelist John Stevens refers in his comments to the two primary arguments established by the Supreme Court which show exceptions to free expression. In the court's decision of the famous 1919 case, *Schenck v. United States*, Justice Oliver Wendell Holmes wrote that the question becomes whether the words used in such circumstances are of such a nature as to create a clear and present danger. That danger might bring about substantive evils that Congress would have a right to prevent. This case, involving the World War I Espionage Act, directly raises the issue of the rights of free expression during a crisis. Justice Holmes had an answer. He wrote, "It is a question of proximity and degree. When a nation is at war many things that might be said in time of peace are such a hindrance to its effort that their utterance will not be endured as long as men fight, and that no court could regard them as protected by a constitutional right" (*Schenck v. U.S.*, 249 U.S. 47, 39 S.Ct. 247, 63 L.Ed. 470, 1919).

In the other case, *Near v. Minnesota* in 1931, the court faced the First Amendment issue of prior restraint. Chief Justice Hughes wrote that the protection is not absolutely unlimited even before publication. He wrote that government might intrude upon free expression in wartime for any obstruction to recruiting services, or the publication of the sailing dates of transports, or the number and location of troops. Holmes also wrote that the government may intrude upon free expression in the case of incitements to acts of violence and attempts to overthrow the government by force (*Near v. Minnesota*, 283 U.S. 667, 51 S.Ct. 625, 75 L.Ed. 1337, 1931).

These same exceptions and the same legal protections of free expression remain in effect today. However, while the mass media may appeal to courts when their access to information is jeopardized, the executive branch uses national security threats as justification for limiting the flow of information. The balance between these competing pressures has shifted during different crises as the historical perspectives in the following section illustrate.

PRESS AND GOVERNMENT
INTERACTION DURING WARTIME

Historically, the role of war correspondent emerged during the Civil War and while writers, photographers, and artists who covered this war enjoyed great freedom, the military attempted to close their access by cutting off the use of telegraph lines. World War I marked the beginning of institutional efforts to control the press. The Woodrow Wilson administration created the Commission on Public Information to disseminate war propaganda and to censor the information available to the press. The commission originated news favorable to the war effort and blacked out that which was not.

During World War II, the United States government profited from the British experiences with censorship policies early in the war; near total censorship prevailed. Correspondents could not be accredited to cover frontline battles unless they submitted all copy to censors. Anything that did not meet the military command's consideration of security was deleted from reports. Newsreels and broadcasts were highly edited. During this period, reporters only rarely broke the guidelines.

President Franklin D. Roosevelt established a separate Office of Censorship, the purpose of which was to suppress unfavorable information—such as private letters that painted a gloomy picture of the war—which might affect public morale. The American censorship policy was "to shield the nation from reality, and to convince the public that the war was being conducted by a command of geniuses" (Knightley 1975, 279). Drew Middleton (1984, 61) has said that one benefit of this institutional censorship was that it enabled the correspondents to be better informed about the war than they were later in Vietnam, since commanders felt they could talk freely with reporters; General Eisenhower took the lead and provided detailed briefings before every operation. In large measure this confidence was justified. Correspondents went along with the official scheme of reporting the war, in part, because they were convinced that it was in the national interest to do so. They saw no sharp demarcation between the role of the press and that of government (Knightley 1975, 276).

Whereas censorship in the two world wars was institutionally organized, in Korea it was generally imposed at the source by senior officers. General Douglas McArthur was a master at publicizing the military's view of operations and also at keeping his mouth shut about impending campaigns. The Vietnam conflict followed a similar pattern. While reporters were free to go where they wished, those who did not have the trust of military officers were given little information. As the Vietnam conflict continued, many officers became convinced that the American public's growing hostility toward the war was really due to biased and inaccurate media accounts. For example, military personnel thought that the news coverage overemphasized the enemy's foray into the U.S. Embassy in accounts which they felt obscured the true dimensions of what should have been recounted as a

1968 victory. Subsequently, according to Drew Middleton (1984, 91), reporters were often verbally attacked by officers for giving false impressions. After American forces had been withdrawn from the Vietnam conflict, many military personnel were embittered by their failure to defeat the Vietnamese. They blamed the course of events on both political maneuvering in Washington and the graphic daily coverage of military events by American correspondents.

To a certain extent, such military critics misunderstood the motives of television journalists. They were not necessarily interested in making political statements in their reports; images of blood and gore were intrinsically newsworthy and, as Middleton pointed out, this coverage of violence and conflict fit the short 30–60–90 second boundaries of the electronic media. However, it was true that correspondents covering the Vietnam War, unlike their colleagues in World War II, resisted military appeals to their patriotism and protection of the national interest (Knightley 1975, 423). As a result, Vietnam was better reported than any other war, but press-government relations deteriorated and journalists' access to military officers was closed.

By the time of the United States' commando-style invasion of the island of Grenada in 1983, the Reagan administration had already initiated numerous policies aimed at reducing media access to domestic, foreign, and military activities, particularly those related to combat. On the domestic side, the administration redefined the guidelines for using the Freedom of Information Act (under these new guidelines, visas were refused to some 8,000 foreign intellectuals, and the flow of controversial films in and out of U.S. borders was inhibited) and attempted to subject its own officials to a lifetime prepublication review. All of these efforts have qualified free access to information, even without the threat of an official war (Abrams 1982, 22–29).

In the Grenada episode the dilemma was real and present. Secretary of Defense Casper W. Weinberger offered this justification for government restrictions: "As public officials, particularly those in national security areas, we are sometimes faced with difficult choices. In this case (Grenada), we came down on the side of trying to provide for the security of the military and the civilian personnel. The unique circumstances of Grenada . . . made it imperative that we rescue the medical students and other civilians before we added noncombatants to the personnel sent to the island" (Weinberger 1983, 4–3). After the invasion, public opinion polls showed support of such government control of the media. Perhaps another index of a changing attitude toward the media is that some 90 percent of recent media-related libel suits that have gone to juries have been decided against the press (Clurman 1983, A27). It is uncertain what these factors indicate for the future of press-government interaction during wartime; but since both modern warfare and media coverage have changed, perhaps it is inevitable that their relationships will also change.

THE ROLES AND RESPONSIBILITIES
OF JOURNALISTS DURING WARTIME

Correspondents learn to respond quickly in reporting wartime events, but they do so under two kinds of constraints—those of official government policies and those dictated by their own values and standards. If the first casualty is truth, then it is often the victim not only of government censorship, but also of the correspondent's identification with a cause that encourages self-censorship even more restrictive than any official constraints (Knightley 1975, 276, 330). Other factors that may influence the character of a journalist's report vary from the nature of the war itself—the issues at stake, the severity of the conflict—to the changing demands of the reporter's medium which, as comments by Bob Faw suggest, can derive from changes in programming format or in the technology used.

The role and responsibilities of journalists have changed over time. As we stated, during World War II elaborate institutional media censorship machinery was in effect and relationships between the military and the press were basically harmonious. Both felt free to talk, even discuss top secret materials, because they had confidence in the effectiveness of censorship policies and had developed a sense of mutual trust. As our panelists state, most World War II correspondents strongly supported war efforts and did not perceive sharp demarcations between their responsibilities and government goals (Knightley 1975, 276). However, such views were not universally shared nor without criticism. Charles Lynch, a Canadian reporter, had a different perspective (Knightley 1975, 333):

We were a propaganda arm of our governments. At the start censors enforced this but by the end of the war we were our own censors.

Lynch and some other reporters felt used in part because much of the time they were physically removed from military activities and were largely dependent on official versions of events as communicated by the military for their stories. Nevertheless, they were cooperative and generally followed government guidelines.

Edward R. Murrow played a very special role in World War II (Smith 1978, 96, 109). As an American journalist in Europe during extremely difficult times, he brought important information about the war to the American public. Murrow had contact with powerful figures so he had relatively little difficulty gaining access to military activities. Murrow believed strongly in his obligation to keep the American public fully informed without jeopardizing war efforts. His oft-cited sense of integrity was reflected in his war coverage.

In his biography of Murrow, Kendrick (1969, 230–40) provides an example of Murrow's self-censorship during wartime. On Sunday, 7 December 1941, the Murrows were invited to the White House for an informal dinner where Murrow and President Roosevelt were to talk informally about Anglo-American relationships. News about Pearl Harbor reached the mainland and the Murrows expected dinner to be canceled but Mrs. Roosevelt insisted they attend. The president was too busy to participate in the dinner but wanted Murrow to stay so he might talk with him. Close to midnight, Murrow met with President Roosevelt who, while clearly fatigued, began telling him the full story surrounding the bombing of Pearl Harbor. President Roosevelt gave Murrow facts and figures. He did not request specifically that their discussions be off-the-record. Murrow agonized over this information. Finally, in an act of self-censorship motivated both by the gravity of the times and by his own values, he decided not to reveal it.

Near-total censorship vanished after World War II; during the Korean and Vietnam conflicts war coverage, in effect, became more dependent upon harmonious relationships between correspondents and the military officers on whom they depended for access to the war and military information. Without the security of institutional censorship, and without a sense of shared national goals, military personnel became more wary of talking to reporters. In recent years, tensions between the military and the media have increased. Some correspondents have indeed become very critical of military activities and agonized over their responsibilities to the public, the war coverage, and to themselves. According to our panelists, the dilemmas are exacerbated by the availability of technology for on-the-spot reporting of the details of war. Correspondents must make instantaneous judgments, and our panelists suggest that under such circumstances they must increasingly rely on their own values and standards.

Journalists must recognize that press-government relationships are still in flux. As Colonel Harry Summers (1983, 4–1) of the Army War College recently commented:

From a strategic perspective, it can be argued that in Vietnam there was too much coverage, in Grenada there was too little. What we must do is to find a balance between these extremes. We are in the process of establishing this balance but let there be no mistake that in a democracy one of the important rights that will be preserved is the right of the citizenry to know what the government is doing and to learn this from a free and independent press.

Winston Churchill may have been right when he said during World War II that "In wartime, truth is so precious that she should be attended by a bodyguard of lies." Whether that bodyguard should depend on organized censorship, the limitation of access, or the mutual cooperation of journalists and the military, is a question that must be asked anew with each new conflict.

PANEL PARTICIPANTS

FENDALL YERXA (*moderator*) recently retired as professor of communications from the University of Washington. Formerly, he had worked for the *New York Times* and ABC News. Also, he served as managing editor of the *New York Herald Tribune* and executive editor and vice-president of the New Journal Newspapers in Wilmington, Delaware.

BOB FAW is a reporter for CBS News. From 1981 to 1983, he covered the political scene in Tel Aviv. He joined CBS News in 1977 after a ten-year career as a television reporter and anchorman in Seattle, Boston, and Chicago. Faw holds the M.S. degree from the London School of Economics and Political Science and has been a fellow of the Center for Policy Study at the University of Chicago.

CLETE ROBERTS began his broadcasting career as a staff member of Trans-Radio Press. During World War II, he served as a war correspondent for ABC. Following the war, he joined the staff of KMPC, Los Angeles, as news director and commentator. Until his death in 1984, Roberts headed his own television documentary unit in Los Angeles and was a news commentator in that city.

JOHN D. STEVENS has been a professor at the University of Michigan since 1967. Formerly, he taught at the University of Wisconsin and Washington State University. He is the author of four books on mass communication, a former head of the History Division of the Association for Education in Journalism and Mass Communication, and is currently chairman of the Department of Communication at the University of Michigan.

*How much should the public know and
when should it know it?*

—FENDALL YERXA

Fendall Yerxa: All of us in the press are interested in the coverage of crises. After all, crisis coverage is our principal business. The central question we have to deal with here is the question of crisis reaction by the media versus people's right to know. To paraphrase Senator Howard Baker's famous question of a few years ago, "How much should the public know and when should it know it?" In one sense, it is a more frightening question for broadcast people than it is for print people because of the greater impact of television, its pervasiveness, and the emotional impact TV carries over print. Secondly, broadcast journalists face greater deadline pressure. Print people do not put out extras anymore and even when they did, they had the luxury of at least a few hours for reflecting on their reactions compared with those of you who see it in minutes and seconds.

In another sense, it seems to me that this question depends somewhat on the nature of the crisis. Journalists are trained to instantly and instinctively react to crisis outbreak. In other words, things break out without full warning—to the breaking news of crisis reporting, to military encouragement, to revolution. Maybe we are not so well trained, or at least not so experienced in dealing with developing crises. For example, it is often said that the press did a comparatively lousy job in preparing us for what eventually happened in Vietnam. We did not react until it broke out. These are issues which can neither be learned nor taught in journalism schools, at least not effectively. So I would like to start perhaps by throwing out that question. How much should the public know and when should it know it? Clete Roberts, who goes back much further than most of us here and has rubbed elbows with more crises than all the rest of us put together, will begin with that question.

*When we are talking about right to know,
we are in fact talking about censorship.*

—CLETE ROBERTS

Clete Roberts: First, I would like to put this in perspective. When we talk about the right to know, we are in fact talking about censorship. In time of war, it usually means military censorship. It has been my good fortune, or my misfortune, to work under military censorship in several wars, several countries.

I learned early about the two kinds of censorship that exist: policy and security censorship. Policy censorship is the kind that avoids embarrassment to the command or in a political situation to the administration, and security censorship avoids giving aid and comfort to the enemy.

War correspondents in World War II were subject to the articles of war just as any member of the armed forces. If we wrote or published anything that aided the enemy, we were in deep trouble. Incidentally, we also agreed that if we came back to the United States we would submit to Washington for censorship over a period of about a year, whatever we wrote.

Of course, no responsible correspondent desires to aid the enemy but no responsible correspondent submits willingly to policy censorship. I had the opportunity, as a correspondent at his headquarters, to learn about policy censorship under perhaps the most skilled public relations man in American military service, General Douglas McArthur. At his command in Australia, and later in New Guinea and the Philippines, great care was taken by the censors to see that we filed nothing that was even vaguely critical of the general. We always argued with these censors and demanded that they show us the security involved in something we had written. Often, the result was a compromise with which both sides could live with a reasonably clear conscience.

Censorship in Korea was much the same. We had only one office to go through — the United Nations Command. Usually they were pretty reasonable. However, I recall a marine general, General Frank Dodd, who was taken prisoner on Koje Island by the North Koreans and the Chinese prisoners of war were incarcerated in the POW camp which he commanded. It was a most embarrassing situation to the commanding general, who was then Matthew Ridgeway. The chief press relations colonel called all the correspondents into a conference in Seoul and told us we would not be permitted to get on the island and if we tried, we would be prevented from working. From our point of view, that was of course, policy censorship. Naturally, we immediately set up a committee and designated one of the group to get to the island. Someone volunteered because as he said, "I'm going home next week anyway, so what the hell." He did get to the island and got his story. He turned himself into the MPs, identified himself, and was promptly taken into custody and brought back to Seoul. Upon his arrival he gave the rest of us his story. As I recall, we made a deal with the censors. We would file the General Dodd story but we would not file the yarn about successfully circumventing the censors. In their view, the latter story would be the most dangerous.

Censorship in Israel during the Suez crisis and the six-day war seemed to be rather reasonable. It was, I thought then, professional. The Israelis had some of the brightest people in the land doing the job and I can recall but one sticky story in the six-day war. It had to do with the capture of some Russian rocket launchers and some Russians who were with the Egyptian army. They may have been operating the rockets or they may have been, as we call them, technical advisors. In any event, we made a deal. We reported the capture of the rocket launchers and the censors deleted the reference to the Russians. That was a fine line, but from our point of view it was policy censorship. From Tel Aviv's point of view, the Russian involvement affected their security.

What I have been talking about, of course, is ancient history. What about the future? In the event of a war, would the media be permitted to function as in the past?

Rather recently the British isolated the press during their invasion and war in the Falkland Islands. They ran the whole show. Could such a condition come to pass in the United States? I do not pretend to know, but if the media does not react, certainly the public will not. Today, we are addressing ourselves, in part, to the public's right to know. Presumably, we shall examine the limitations that might be put on that right in time of crisis, but I feel we should examine closely that right as it exists in time of so-called normalcy.

Perhaps we should ask ourselves if there is any real point to these discussions in view of the fact that in some future crisis, we may find ourselves working under ground rules that would make it virtually impossible to function as responsible correspondents. It has been observed that the Vietnam conflict may well have been the last open war for the press. It may well have been. If our government can lay down ground rules for peacetime that limit the press function in this country, why would we be surprised to see the Pentagon and the administration adopt the tactics now practiced by Russia in Afganistan, where a war is under way that is poorly reported simply because the press really cannot get in. It must be discussed today and I hope we find some answers.

Broadcasting technology has made censorship a whole different kind of problem.
— JOHN STEVENS

John Stevens: When we talk about the legal bearing of this in the twentieth century, we have to harken back to the immediate post–World War I decision, the *Schenck* decision. This decision said that when a nation is at war, many things that might be said in time of peace are such a hindrance to its effort that their utterance will not be endured as long as men fight and that no court could regard them as protected by a constitutional right. Those words have been quoted in every legal decision which has in any way upheld the censorship control of the press. Those words were cited as at least dicta, if not the major authority, in the famous *Near v. Minnesota* decision in 1931. *Near v. Minnesota* eliminated prior restraint, but on the other hand, it also left some big loopholes, which have shown up in cases like the Pentagon Papers.

I was interested in what Clete said, that Vietnam may have been our last open war. It reminded me of a quotation from Richard Harding Davis, that knight errant who spent the early twentieth century roaming the world hunting for wars, finding them usually, posing in the front of them with a patch over his eye, and writing magnificent prose. His remark when covering World War I was that it was a modern war and that we would never again have the kind of situation that we had in the Spanish-American War, where the press really had free reign. It may be a relative matter. Broadcasting technology has made censorship a whole different kind of problem. Compare this to the impact of transmissions via satellites. New technologies have no respect for political boundaries. These are only some of the issues for the future.

Fendall Yerxa: Bob Faw, you have the contemporary view, perhaps a little more than the rest of us. What are your reflections on how much should the people know and when should they know it?

"It takes two to speak the truth, one to speak and another to hear." That quotation hung on a wall in [Ed Murrow's office].
— BOB FAW

Bob Faw: Let me try to raise a few questions about the issue of whether or not the American public has a right to know everything in times of crisis. It would be tempting to say yes, but it would also be wrong, certainly wrong when it comes to the borders in Israel. For one thing, the ground rules are totally different. There is no First Amendment guarantee and while Israelis demand a vigorous and an outspoken press, they know that when it comes to issues of security the Israeli public does not have the right to know everything. Logically it follows that if they don't, then the American public being told about Israel will not either.

Secondly, Israeli censorship makes sure that the American public does not know everything. When it comes to military affairs, every word is scripted, every picture must be submitted to and approved by an army censor. That procedure can be arbitrary, it can be enlightening, it can be irrational, but the fact is it nearly always works.

Ask yourself just this summer how many times you saw pictures, detailed photographs, of the fighter planes which bombed Beirut. Those planes were made in America by and large. The answer is that you did not see them, even though you had a right to because a lot of them had been paid for with American tax dollars. What censorship, official censorship, does not limit, self-censorship certainly does.

Until Lebanon, Israeli wars were wars of survival. Everyone in the country knew it and acted accordingly. As one of Israel's toughest and best military reporters put it, "We do not write all we know and we see. Who does?" The different rules mean a lot of things but it certainly means that less news gets back to the so-called American public. Call it, if you will, expectations. When the subject is Israel, the public expects something different, something more, something better. It is partly Israel's fault. Ben-Gurion once said, "We Israelis are entitled to cling to the conviction that merely to be like all other people is not enough." Israel's survival never has been enough. The goal from the beginning has not been just to create a state where Jews could live but to have the special kind of place.

Before 1967, when Israel was tiny and beleaguered, things were different. The 1967 war changed all that, Israel became a conqueror which sacked mayors, tore down houses, exiled dissidents, and even killed demonstrators. When it started doing that it lost some of its moral stature. One of its friends wrote, "It became, like a lot of other nations, better than most, maybe worse than none, but certainly worse than measured against what it had once been and what it had once disclaimed."

The measuring business in the news sense, again, got in the way this summer. Invade Lebanon, bomb civilian areas, that was not the sort of thing Israel was expected to do. Outrage grew. The same outrage, I point out, which was not directed at other countries. For example, in 1970 about 30,000 members of the Palestine Liberation Organization were slaughtered by King Hussein in Jordan. Very little attention was devoted to that in the media, likewise last year when Syria's president virtually wiped out an entire town to destroy some political opposition. Neither of those slaughters were newsworthy enough to make the cover of *Time* or *Newsweek* or the nightly network broadcast.

The American public should go back to the original question. Does it have a right to know everything that it can? But I also think that it has a right, maybe an obligation to know that on some subjects, like Israel, it is seeing through rose-colored glasses, or face-hardened, or cracked, but glasses none the less. Given that the question is what kind of job we in the electronic media are doing, and my impression is that when it comes to the Middle East, the job has not been very good. Partly it is the censorship I mentioned, partly it is a matter of access. Mostly, though, the performance has fallen short because of the nature of the beast. Perhaps a forty-five-second report is accurate because it shows what happens for a few seconds, but it is not complete or fair because it does not show what happened before.

An American audience watching Israeli soldiers club Arab demonstrators might, and hopefully does, hear the background that is given in an accompanying script. But most people will rarely hear or comprehend the script because what they are seeing is just too strong. The visual does not just warp the rest, it often obliterates it. What gets lost is not the subtlety of the nuance; what gets lost day after day is the context. So much so that I am persuaded that while television can present the horror and the emotion of war better than any other medium, it cannot explain what is happening or why or the significance of the coverage. Pictures simply get in the way; the images are just too strong. As a result, only a part of the reality is conveyed, only part of the public right to know is met. I mention all of this to suggest that the question before this panel is not quite as simple as it seems. The public has a right to know, it also has an obligation to know, but the information it is presented can be distorted not only by those who gather it but by those who receive it as well.

In times of crisis, truth is not the only casualty. For Israel all times are times of crisis, and so the right to know travels on a two-way street. As Thoreau said, "It takes two to speak the truth, one to speak and another to hear." That quotation hung on a wall in an office in New York. It was Ed Murrow's office.

Fendall Yerxa: Bob, you have been talking about self-restraint on the part of the press to keep things off the air that maybe should not be shown in times of crisis. Do you find yourself frustrated, perhaps from time to time, when you have only two minutes to tell a story like Murrow's famous broadcast from Buchenwald where on the radio he was able to enthrall his audience for twenty minutes?

Bob Faw: It is a frustration that you do not get away from and the only satisfaction is hoping that in the few minutes you had, you did more than the competition does. Sometimes that is a pretty phony yardstick. It is a daily frustration; there is no way around it. After ten years of this kind of thing, an entire generation of viewers have become accustomed to that. Their attention span is so limited, the perception of management is so limited, that they rarely stretch out those few minutes. Obviously, there are long pieces from time to time on all the broadcasts, but the expectation is that you have to keep it short, you have to keep it relatively simple because otherwise the audience will drift away. The loser in that regard is the public.

Fendall Yerxa: Are you suggesting that we in journalism have gotten so used to covering crises that perhaps we are generating a little, almost, in order to keep our audience?

Bob Faw: Yes and no in part. Perhaps it is indirect when night after night we come back and tell New York we have good pictures today from the West Bank. The riots were really bloody today. That tends to invest the event with a little more importance, if you will, than if we say there were two deaths but we did not get any pictures. If there are not any pictures, it did not happen and so in that sense merely the selection process can be distorted. It is an ongoing problem that has always been there. My concern is what happens night after night when the visual is so strong that it tends to overwhelm what accompanies it.

Clete Roberts: It is agreed that World War I would have ended a lot sooner if there had been some correspondents over there to report that event. Phillip Knightley, who wrote *The First Casualty*, pointed out that when we entered the war and sent correspondents over, on the first boat was Richard Harding Davis. Davis had been there a little while and had thrown up his hands and came home, saying he could not report it. If he could have and if others could have reported the death in the trenches, the useless waste of life, then maybe the history of off-the-street news would have been different and maybe there would not have been a Versailles treaty or even a Hitler.

Fendall Yerxa: I want to reflect on an episode in print journalism which occurred at a crucial time in our history where if it had gone the other way, history might have been written a little bit differently. This raises the question about the wisdom of some journalists in reaction to crisis.

Remember the Tonkin Gulf episode and the Tonkin Gulf resolution which Lyndon Johnson so carefully prepared to take up to the Hill and how it swept through with virtually no opposition whatsoever. I happened to be the Washington news editor that night and the reporter who was covering the Hill and the passage of that resolution came back to the office afterwards and wrote the spot story on the passage of the resolution. He then came to me and said that we had to have a "fuelhead." A fuelhead in the *New York Times* is a news analysis, labeled as such. This was late in the evening and we had to have a fuelhead to point out that the Congress had given Lyndon Johnson a blank check to take this country to war. We used our best efforts to prevail on New York to give us the space and the time and permission to go ahead and write that story. It was denied. It was denied because of space considerations and time pressures and so forth, but for whatever reason, I think it was a gross error in judgment. It was not judgment that was made by politicians, not censorship by officialdom, but censorship by ourselves.

Clete Roberts: I agree the right to know has to be respected. The public has to be constantly reminded it has that right and it should not be restricted in any way except when we print or publicize something which aids and comforts an enemy. The thing that worries all of us is who are these people who classify this as a secret? Usually it is people who are thinking first, in matters of policy, and of not embarrassing whomever is in command. We have to maintain an adversary relationship with those people, we have to question them all the time and not worry about whether or not we are popular with them. After all, journalism is not a popularity contest.

Fendall Yerxa: Another problem related to this is the need to reach our definition of what constitutes a crisis. We have been talking about some very

very obvious ones here—outbreaks and turning points in wars—but there are other kinds of crises which run just as deep when it concerns the public's right to know. A case in point is the Pentagon Papers case. As you know, the *Times* worked on the Pentagon Papers case. When the first story on the Pentagon Papers was published in the Sunday edition in June 1971 it attracted so little attention the *New York Times* was fearful it had labored mightily and brought forth a mouse. Nobody paid any attention to it. As a matter of fact, Melvin Laird, who was then the secretary of defense, called John Mitchell in the morning and said, "I have to go on 'Meet the Press' or 'Face the Nation' and I am going to be asked about this thing. What am I going to say?" "All you have to say Melvin, is that the matter has been turned over to the Justice Department for investigation and that you will have no further comment." Melvin Laird went on the program. Normally, there are usually about twenty questions asked on one of those programs. Nobody had anything to say about the Pentagon Papers case, in spite of the fact that one of the members of the panel was a *New York Times* reporter. As a matter of fact, it did not become a crisis until a couple of days later when the government asked the *Times* to cease and desist and then finally went to court. That is what made it a crisis story but not until then.

Clete Roberts: Maybe the values of our society are such that the public is not really interested in the crises we think are vital. But again, the challenge comes back to us. How can the media reach out and get the public's attention?

Media, Morality, and the Public

> . . . the domain of the mass media today is an ethical jungle in which pragmatism is king, agreed principles as to daily practice are few, many of the inhabitants pride themselves on the anarchy of their surroundings.
>
> HODDING CARTER III
> Chief Correspondent, "Inside
> Story," from Bruce M. Swain,
> *Reporters' Ethics, 1978*

JOURNALISTS have shown only intermittent interest in developing ethical guidelines, even though the need has always been there. Their reluctance today has been for several reasons: they wanted freedom to act in crisis and noncrisis situations, they feared judges would make guidelines into a rule of law, and they preferred self-enforced professional standards. The journalists' modes of conduct have not been without complaint and attempted correction. At the turn of the century, muckraker Will Irwin indicted the American newspaper business in *Collier's Magazine* for its numerous ethical faults. More recently, Hodding Carter pointed out journalists still have few principles in common and their actions are usually guided by pragmatic rather than moral or philosophical concerns.

The earliest media professional code of ethics of some sixty years ago established the minimal criteria of accuracy and truth. To these, in 1947 the Commission on Freedom of the Press added a significant elaboration by directing journalists to "give a truthful and accurate account of the day's events in a context which gives them meaning." Such generally phrased requirements have offered little guidance or control in an era of heightened demands for media accountability. A list of the significant events of these years—the Bay of Pigs, the Vietnam War, the Pentagon Papers, the Wa-

69

tergate break-in—charts a gradual change in the relationships between government, press, and public. On the one hand, the relationship between government and mass media has changed from mutual cooperation to legitimate skepticism and, at times, to barely concealed antagonism. When government officials lied to journalists, who then relayed the misinformation to the public, many reporters felt betrayed and as a result became more adversarial toward the federal government. This, in effect, gave reporters a new freedom to doggedly pursue hints of government wrongdoing wherever they led, and they sometimes led to startling places. In their desire to expose wrongdoing, journalists sometimes did wrong; consequently, public suspicion of the integrity of the media has also grown.

The reporter's role is that of a communicator, fulfilling a vital function in a healthy democracy by seeking the truth and relaying it accurately and in depth. The importance of this role is recognized in its unique protection under the First Amendment. In practice, however, journalistic "truth" can be an ambiguous even elusive matter, since in its production the journalist is subject to various pressures not the least of which is the desire to succeed professionally in a system which rewards visibility—the top story, the scoop. Every time a reporter makes a choice—which words or pictures or which sources to use—his or her personal integrity is tested. Moreover, the drive to discover *the* story that will lead the front page or evening news as well as scoop the opposition offers the temptation to push so hard as to create, by the contagion of this effort alone, political or social issues out of thin air. Under these circumstances, the "rights" of the press under the First Amendment can be thrown into question.

Generally, the public has to trust the mass media to provide factual accounts of events. Because of this, the public has a right to expect at the very least that a story is produced and presented correctly. They must be able to assume that a story is free from conflicts of interest, that it does not victimize the innocent, and that it is fact. Moreover, if the story is televised, they should be able to expect that it is appropriately presented for family viewing. In essence, the public must be able to respect the media—respect the integrity of the journalists' product and respect the traditions of journalism and broadcasting as carriers of information and leaders of public opinion. But reporters, producers, and others must earn such respect in their practice. By and large, the public's trust and respect has not been misplaced, but on occasion it has been put under strain. Consequently, we will examine how the American mass media grapple with their own ethical dilemmas.

REPORTERS AS NEWSGATHERERS

It is fair to assume that reporters want to serve the truth, yet they face substantial obstacles. Broadcasts and newspapers must be filled daily and reporters must find something that is novel, recent, or exciting from the seemingly unending stream of news stories that reach their desks. Modern journalism has been called "history in a hurry." Under these conditions, it is difficult to provide both precise and representative stories, particularly when they have to fit a two-minute or less television slot or a compacted newspaper article. Where do reporters go to find significant stories? How do they develop and maintain contacts with busy, elusive, and prominent news makers?

Reporters must reconcile a number of conflicting interests in their use of sources in gathering the news. As Bruce M. Swain (1978, 3) warned, "a reporter may be influenced by loyalties engendered by cooperation on previous stories, personal philosophies, friendships, investments, outside jobs, or the lure of being considered an expert or an insider." In a way, the source might be said to dictate the story. Often the reporter in the rush to do a job under deadline will turn to sources used in previous stories rather than hunt out new ones. The information might be less reliable—it might even be totally wrong—but it is used because it is easy to obtain. Under other circumstances the journalist might suppress a story entirely in order to preserve the source for future information. And if the source, who is likely to be a newsworthy person, is a friend, the reporter might very well be faced by a conflict of interest. As well as coping with these delicate problems, the reporters must constantly deal with people who attempt to influence them with such subtle bribes as news tips, favors, or a shrewd use of social events. Journalists must tread a precarious path in maintaining their access to information and sources while retaining their autonomy and integrity.

Some threats to journalistic integrity are obvious—the temptations of economic gain or outside employment, for example. The most notorious media scandals have involved payoffs and favors, and various media codes of ethics now explicitly state that reporters should not accept gifts, travel, special treatment, jobs, and the like from outside interests. Other threats, however, are less easy to identify. Our panel moderator, Fred Friendly, offers one example when he asks the others what they would do when the source for their story is a former classmate and business associate. The responses of the panel vary, but all recognize the need for self-examination and perspective under such circumstances.

Eliminating or avoiding all such influences is not easy. The broader issue is, of course, How far will reporters go to get a story? How important is confidentiality of sources? Should a reporter decide the rightness or wrongness of stories? Fred Friendly poses this in specific terms when he asks panelists if they would lie, steal, or deceive to obtain a story. Some of the panelists admit that they might, depending on the situation. However, as Clifford G. Christians and his coauthors (1983, 48) pointed out, "Outright deceit occurs infrequently in newswriting but deception in newsgathering is a persistent temptation because it often facilitates the process of securing information." What are some of the specific dilemmas media professionals face in news gathering and how do they solve them?

ETHICAL DILEMMAS IN NEWS GATHERING

Every day reporters work with sources who agree to talk only "off the record" or under the guarantee of confidentiality. Once information is taken off the record, the reporter is obligated by personal honor not to reveal the identity of the source. Implicit in this promise of confidentiality is the journalists' conviction that if they don't protect their sources, no one will have faith in them; promises must be kept to secure the public's trust. The legal status of this promise varies from state to state and judge to judge (Swain 1978, 52). But the Supreme Court has ruled that a journalist is not guaranteed constitutional protection from grand jury requests to reveal sources. The reporter's uncertain legal position is only one difficulty raised by this practice. Often journalists have good reasons to protect sources of information, but there are dangers in doing so. Unless they are very careful, they can be co-opted into suppressing news or deceived into conveying misinformation. Also, the practice itself lays them open to the accusation that they abuse this "veil of secrecy" in order to become makers, rather than reporters, of policy. In each case, reporters must decide whether information from their sources is valuable enough for them to take these risks. Arthur Thomason of the *St. Louis Globe Democrat* has his own personal rule. He states, "if something is going to be off the record there has got to be some sort of equalizer, something that is going on the record that will let the public know what is happening." The reporter's task is to strike a balance between reporting a story, protecting the general welfare of the source, and anticipating the possible consequences of the story (Swain 1978, 51, 57).

Perhaps the most notorious case involving confidentiality of sources was the investigation of the Watergate break-in and subsequent events. The two *Washington Post* reporters, Bob Woodward and Carl Bernstein, zealously guarded the anonymity of their informant "Deep Throat" and would not reveal the name even to their editors. During the unfolding of this significant story, which eventually led to the prosecution of government officials and resignation of the president of the United States, the reporters steadfastly refused to reveal the source. *Washington Post* editors, to insure that information from the source was reliable, insisted that Woodward and Bernstein have two independent verifications of all information that was published. The dilemma faced by the two reporters epitomizes that of all users of "personal" sources—that of assessing the reliability and validity of information without breaking the pledge of confidentiality. There are no easy solutions to this problem, and reporters approach these problems differently depending on the situation.

Our panelists, for example, when asked by Fred Friendly how they would deal with a source who offered dramatic, strategic information while demanding confidentiality, give various responses. Bob Faw and others say that until they know substantial details, they will keep the source confidential, even from editors or producers. Other panelists are not so certain.

A related problem discussed by our panel places great demands on reporters' subtlety and judgment. When offered a news leak, reporters must decide what to make of the leakers and their motives. As one reporter of the *Wall Street Journal* has said, "The best bribe is always a lead on a better story" (Swain 1978, 20). Information leads are not always motivated by altruism; the informant usually may have an ax to grind and the reporter must discover what it is in order to judge the reliability of the leak. Reporters can bluff, suggesting that they have more information than they actually do, or they may use information already acquired as leverage.

Other difficult and delicate ethical problems occur when reporters collaborate with official agencies. Under such circumstances, they are faced with the question of whether the ends justify the means. Tom Goldstein (1984, 23) explored the implications of this kind of collaboration in his discussion of a recent investigation of a Florida politician accused of corruption. The politician confided in a reporter about his sexual escapades with prostitutes supplied by a contractor seeking county business. He asked her to keep this information off the record, but instead she informed the prosecutor's office and became an active participant in gathering evidence and arranging the politician's arrest. Investigators allowed the reporter to accompany them as they staked out the politician, provided that she held the story until the case was complete. The extent of this reporter's cooperation was unusual but not unique and raises the question of just how far journalists should go to obtain their stories. Clearly, most newspeople believe that journalists should not willingly reveal information obtained in confidence, but they also feel they have a responsibility to inform officials of illegal activities. The dilemma is how to balance these pressures. Goldstein noted that few news organizations have established policies about collaboration between journalists and law enforcement agencies; consequently, the reporter must exercise his or her judgment about the situation and the relationship with investigators. The limits are largely determined on a case-by-case basis (Goldstein 1984, 29).

The question still remains, "How far will a reporter go to get a story?" The dilemmas in working with sources and collaborating with official agencies cover only a small part of what reporters do to obtain a story. Other practices are even more questionable — dirty tricks and sloppy research techniques (Lewis 1983). For example, recent television exposés have been criticized for their "ambush interview" technique by which television crews working on an investigation will approach a subject without warning and demand answers to questions (*America* 1981, 375). The interviewee is taken aback and either refuses to answer or offers answers so incoherent as to be self-damning. These responses often create the appearance of guilt which the broadcasters may exploit. Such practices, while they are powerfully effective in the short term, once exposed provide ammunition for media critics and call media ethics and social responsibility into question.

THE PUBLIC PERCEPTION

If recent public opinion polls are correct, the press has alienated itself from the very public it serves as a constituency. The public often now sees the press as an agent of power, untrustworthy and unreliable. Outrageous stories, dirty tricks, and insensitive reporting have all played their part in this. Ironically, many journalistic excesses represent the same kind of behavior exposed and condemned by the press itself during the Watergate era. The press deplored the clandestine photographing and bugging of political radicals during the sixties and seventies, and yet newspapers and broadcasting stations have employed the same devices themselves. CBS occasionally uses a hidden camera in preparing segments of "60 Minutes"; and it was only a few years ago that reporters for the *Chicago Sun Times* opened a phony tavern, the Mirage, and photographed and recorded city officials for weeks in an attempt to gain evidence of corruption among the city building and fire inspectors.

While the press has done a good job in sensitizing the public to ethical dilemmas and conflicts of interest in government, it has done less well in acknowledging or reporting its own behavioral lapses. A double standard seems to operate whereby the evening news might prominently report a leading official's infringement of the law but ignore any ethical or legal violations on the part of reporters. How can the public trust a mass media often blind to its own failings?

The solution, of course, lies in the integrity of journalistic practices. If journalists and broadcasters made correct ethical decisions, there would be no violations to report. But this, as is clear, is fraught with difficulties — the reporter must make such decisions by weighing the conflicting demands imposed by the rights of any one individual or group and the rights of others. As our panel discussion reveals, each media employee has multiple, conflicting obligations — to himself/herself, to employers, to professional colleagues, and to society. Working journalists might feel the tug of these obligations in different proportions than, for example, media executives, but they apply to both. Any decision inevitably favors one set of priorities over the others, and the difficulty is in deciding where the first loyalty lies. Finally, they have to rely on their own judgment and integrity, saying with panelist Andy Ludlum, "I only know my own integrity."

This country has always needed accounts of our common public life, enlightened consumer information, and even forms of entertainment with some redeeming value, and the ethical integrity of the media which offered them has been of primary importance. Now, however, in the so-called information age, when newspapers, magazines, radio and television have exploited the new technology to pervade our lives as never before, the need for ethical and socially responsible media behavior is even more acute. Just how socially responsible will this information-age press be to its first constituency — the public?

PANEL PARTICIPANTS

FRED FRIENDLY (*moderator*) is the Edward R. Murrow Professor Emeritus at the Columbia University Graduate School of Journalism and Director of the Columbia University Seminars on Media and Society. He collaborated with Murrow on the CBS radio series "Hear It Now" and the television series "See It Now." Friendly ended his network career with two years as president of CBS News. He resigned in 1966 to join the faculty at Columbia and to become a consultant to the Ford Foundation.

KENNETH EIKENBERRY is the fourteenth attorney general of the State of Washington. After receiving his degree from the University of Washington Law School, he spent two years as a special agent for the FBI and six years as deputy prosecuting attorney for King County. He has served as vice-president of the Western Conference of Attorney Generals.

BOB FAW is a reporter for CBS News. From 1981–1983 he covered the political scene in Tel Aviv. He joined CBS News in 1977 after a ten-year career as a television reporter and anchorman in Seattle, Boston, and Chicago. Faw holds the M.S. degree from the London School of Economics and has been a fellow of the Center for Policy Study at the University of Chicago.

CAROL JANSON is a reporter for the ABC affiliate KXLY, Spokane.

ANDY LUDLUM was managing editor of CBS affiliate KIRO, Seattle. He has been with the station for the past five years. Previously, Ludlum worked at KXRX, San Jose.

ROBERT McNICHOLS has been chief judge of the United States District Court for Eastern Washington since 1979. He attended law school at Gonzaga University and then spent two years as deputy prosecuting attorney for Spokane County. Judge McNichols is a fellow of the American College of Trial Lawyers.

DEAN MELL was president of the Radio Television News Directors Association. He has been news director at KHQ-AM/FM TV, Spokane, since 1973. Prior to joining the station, Mell spent eleven years with NBC News in San Francisco and New York.

SIG MICKELSON was CBS's chief executive for news and public affairs from 1951–1961. He also served as vice-president of Time, Incorporated; chairman of the Editorial Department, Northwestern University; president of Radio Free Europe; and executive director of the Center for Communications, San Diego State University.

ARVAL MORRIS is a scholar in constitutional law at the University of Washington Law School. He is the author of two books and numerous articles on the U.S. Constitution and legal theory. Morris has appeared before the U.S. Supreme Court and has been a Fulbright lecturer and visiting professor in West Germany and at Oxford.

RICHARD SALANT is senior advisor to NBC and a former vice-chairman of the National Broadcasting Company. He was twice president of CBS News (from 1961–1964 and 1966–1979) and served as vice-president of Corporate Affairs. Salant holds the LL.B. degree from Harvard.

BARRY SERAFIN has covered the Washington, D.C., scene for ABC News since 1979. He began his career in broadcasting while a student at Washington State University. Before joining ABC, Serafin was with CBS in St. Louis and Washington, D.C. He covered the Iranian embassy siege in Iran for ABC News.

JOHN SHARNIK retired from CBS News in 1982 as senior executive producer of Prime-Time Documentaries. From 1975–1977, he served as CBS News vice-president and director, Public Affairs Broadcasts. Previously, he was an editor of the *New York Times* Sunday Department.

JOHN D. STEVENS has been professor of communication at the University of Michigan since 1967. He is the author of four books on mass communication and a former head of the History Division of the Association for Education in Journalism and Mass Communication.

KAY WIGHT is vice-president, Compliance and Administration, with CBS Sports. She has held a variety of positions with the network since joining CBS in 1963. Wight holds numerous awards from broadcast and civic groups.

FENDALL YERXA recently retired as professor of communications from the University of Washington. Formerly, he had worked for the *New York Times* and ABC News. He also served as managing editor of the *New York Herald Tribune* and executive editor and vice-president of the *New Journal Newspapers* in Wilmington, Delaware.

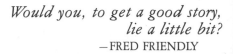

Would you, to get a good story,
lie a little bit?
— FRED FRIENDLY

Fred Friendly: It is very easy to be a journalist, judge, or prosecutor when everything goes the way it is supposed to but it is very hard to do it when the roof falls in. It is very hard to do it whether you are in southern Nebraska where I once was when the roof fell in — there was a terrible murder of six people — or during the tough times of Vietnam or Korea. That is what journalists are trained to think about and to prepare for, and that was something always on the mind of the man whom we are here to honor these few days.

So, we begin with you Carol Janson. I want you to imagine that you no longer are in Spokane but in New York or Washington. Would you, to get a good story, lie a little bit?

No.
— CAROL JANSON

Carol Janson: No.

Fred Friendly: Would you steal?

Carol Janson: No.

Fred Friendly: Judge McNichols, in your line of work, would you ever fabricate or steal a tiny document, a piece of paper or something?

. . . you might create by inference for a
proper purpose — an impression that was
not accurate.
— ROBERT McNICHOLS

Judge McNichols: You are talking about white lies, not stealing. Once in a while, you might create by inference for a proper purpose — an impression that was not accurate.

Fred Friendly: Interesting, you are willing to be a little more permissive than my friends in journalism. How about you, Mr. Faw?

I have lied.
—BOB FAW

Bob Faw: I have lied.

Fred Friendly: You have lied. What is the matter with her? (Points to Janson.) She is not educated?

Bob Faw: Maybe she is more successful doing it the way she does.

Fred Friendly: Well, she is just beginning. Here is what happens, Ms. Janson. You are sitting in your office in the news room at the Federal Broadcasting Corporation and the phone rings. The caller says, I have watched you on the tube and I think you are terrific. I like your work and I have a good story for you. Will you meet me in the park at Lafayette Square opposite the White House? Just you. Will you meet me?

Carol Janson: I would want to know a little more.

Fred Friendly: I cannot tell you very much more except that I work at the State Department and you will not be wasting your time. Will you meet me?

Carol Janson: Yes.

Fred Friendly: There we are out on the bench and I tell you I do not know much about your business but I have been reading *All the President's Men*, I know about the Pentagon Papers, and I watch "60 Minutes." Tell me, can I be your source?

Carol Janson: Yes.

Fred Friendly: You cannot tell anybody who I am. Eventually, I want you to put this on the air or in your newspaper but you cannot tell anybody where you got it. Do you agree to that?

Carol Janson: Yes.

Fred Friendly: Word of honor?

Carol Janson: Word of honor.

Fred Friendly: Now let me tell you what is going on in the world. It is 1994 and we are in the middle of another oil crunch brought on by an embargo. Gasoline, if you can get it, is eight dollars a gallon and you have to stand in line for five hours to get four gallons. There is an international and national depression just like there was in 1932. One of the by-products of petroleum is fertilizer so there is also an international famine. Unemployment is at 24 million people in the United States and inflation is increasing geometrically annually. The country is in the worst mess since the 1930s. The president of the United States, a great woman, is under great pressure to do something and so is the Congress. There are riots in some of the cities, there is a demand for action and no one knows what to do.

Now we are back on the park bench with you and the source. This is what he tells you: Our country is about to make a terrible mistake. You know about those twenty to thirty hostages taken by student terrorists who are holed up at the consulate in the town outside of Madre. This is not a Middle East situation, it could be South America, Africa, or Asia; the country is Madre. You know this situation is true because you have been hearing about it every night on television and in the newspapers. Well, the source tells you we are going to go into Madre and rescue the hostages. But that is only the front. What we are really going to do is rescue the hostages, but we are also going to stay in Madre. Madre is an oil-producing country, the fourth largest, and we are going to take over Madre after we liberate the prisoners. We are going to stay in there and within five days we expect to be pumping fuel into tankers which are now 500 miles from Madre but on their way. Good story?

Carol Janson: A wonderful story.

Fred Friendly: Do you want to ask me anything else? Do you want to ask me when it is going to happen?

Carol Janson: When?

Fred Friendly: I really do not know but I think within forty-eight hours.

Carol Janson: Who is involved?

Fred Friendly: Marines, air force, army special strike force, swat team, all ready to go. It is just between us now. He tells you all about it, lays out the blueprint, and so forth. Is that good enough for you? What else do you want?

Carol Janson: Other sources.

Fred Friendly: Why?

Carol Janson: Because this person could have his reasons for saying this to me.

Fred Friendly: He told you his reasons—he does not want the country to make another terrible, dreadful mistake, not another Tonkin Gulf, not another Bay of Pigs.

Carol Janson: But that is only what he says.

Fred Friendly: What are you going to ask him Mr. Faw?

Bob Faw: I would ask to see, if I could, anything in black and white and I would just keep listening.

Fred Friendly: But the first threshold question was, am I your source?

Bob Faw: If I am bound by that . . .

Fred Friendly: You are bound by that. Are you going to talk to your producer on the nightly news at this stage?

Bob Faw: At this stage, probably not, depending on who the producer is.

Fred Friendly: The producer is Mr. Sharnik. Mr. Sharnik you were once in a job like that. Do you want your reporters out there sitting on park benches with sources?

I would like to have my reporters requiring a little more before they agree to meet strange men in parks.
                                                    — JOHN SHARNIK

John Sharnik: Not on the strength of what I heard being offered. I would like to have my reporters requiring a little more before they agree to meet strange men in parks.

Fred Friendly: What would you like them to ask?

John Sharnik: I would like them to have asked for a little more evidence than was given to them.

Fred Friendly: I am going to make this harder for you, Mr. Sharnik. When they meet in the park bench, the source turns out to be a Washington State

University classmate, a Phi Beta Kappa person, president of the student government, a marvelous person you have not seen in ten years since he has gone to the State Department and risen and you have become a rising star in television.

John Sharnik: I would certainly have asked him what are the balancing considerations? For example, the lives of the hostages.

Fred Friendly: We are not ready for that yet, Mr. Sharnik. You are a gate-keeper. We are just probing right now.

Mr. Mell, I know you operate in Spokane but I also know you are president of the Radio/Television News Directors. What do you think of Carol Janson's promise not to reveal her sources?

> *I do not think that is a*
> *promise you give so early . . .*
> —DEAN MELL

Dean Mell: I do not think that is a promise you give so early but I would agree with her.

Fred Friendly: Mr. Ludlum, you are not the reporter, you are a managing editor. Faw, Serafin, and Janson are the reporters out there on the firing line. They have also seen the glint in the source's eye that he is going to go someplace else.

> *I want to know more about*
> *the source from the reporter.*
> —ANDY LUDLUM

Andy Ludlum: As a managing editor, I do not want to put my, whatever, on the line. I do not know whether that source is any good. I want to know more about the source from the reporter.

Fred Friendly: Why don't you have that conversation with Mr. Faw? Mr. Faw comes in and says, "I am working on this story, I am a long way away from going with it, but I am working on it. I want you to know that." What are you going to ask him?

Andy Ludlum: Who is the source?

Bob Faw: Somebody I must trust and who seems to have a responsible job. It is early, I need more time and there is enough here to at least warrant another conversation. This may be a total dead end and then maybe not but what else have I got to do? If the source is right, then let us take some time and do it.

Andy Ludlum: How are you going to confirm it?

Bob Faw: I do not know yet, it is early. I simply wanted you to know what is involved here and that is all I want you to know at this point.

Fred Friendly: Mr. Serafin, Miss Janson, are you going to tell him the source?

Andy Ludlum: I am going to ask.

Fred Friendly: But you just got told no soap. What about you, Mr. Yerxa? Fendall was at the *New York Times* at the time of the Bay of Pigs. I am going to make you the editor, it is your newspaper. We will change the story slightly. Are you going to let these three fine reporters investigate the story without telling you the source?

You do not give your confidence lightly.
—FENDALL YERXA

Fendall Yerxa: No, the reporter who works for me is going out to the park bench and tell the source that he is not just Bob Faw. You knew before you went out there that you are not Bob Faw, you are CBS or you are the *New York Times*. We know that nowadays you do not give your confidence to any source especially on heavy stuff like this. You do not give your confidence lightly.

Bob Faw: Now wait just a minute here. This person has been given absolutely nothing. I merely had a preliminary conversation and all I agreed to do was not tell anyone who I had spoken with. It is so early in the game that the odds here may be great but the payoff could be enormous. We have to look into it, and all I want you to know is that this is involved.

Fendall Yerxa: That sounds fine but the trouble is that you gave your confidence to this source before he told you anything and you have given your confidence down the line for anything he tells you thereafter. I do not think you can do that.

Fred Friendly: Then why don't you trust him to do this story? He has a great record. He has done this a half a dozen times and did not even tell you the other times. This one is so big that he is trusting you, he is telling you and you are putting a wet towel over him. Are you going to dry up the source with a wet towel? Forgive the metaphor. What about you, Mr. Salant, from the high reaches of news division. How do you want your Sharniks, your Ludlums acting? Do you want them to demand the source?

. . . there are very tricky grounds in assuring confidentiality of sources.

—RICHARD SALANT

Richard Salant: I would try to impress my associates that there are very tricky grounds in assuring confidentiality of sources.

Fred Friendly: Mr. Salant, this is a big story. They want to know if they can get going on this story. Are you going to let them go or not?

Richard Salant: I would say no, you cannot give that assurance unless you are prepared to go to jail. This is one of the difficulties of confidential sources. We cannot give them lightly because we may not be able to stick to them. I would suggest to Mr. Serafin that what he ought to do is say he will do his best to keep the source confidential but he is not absolutely sure he can do it. But, we are not going to go with the story on the basis of what this person tells us anyway. He is just a reason to go check with other people and find out if it is true.

. . . you are going to have to go to court and be required to disclose your source . . .

—BARRY SERAFIN

Barry Serafin: I understand that but sooner or later in this kind of volatile situation somebody is going to get mad and something is going to happen. There is a pretty good chance you are going to have to go to court and be required to disclose your source and you are going to say no.

Fred Friendly: Let's get down to case history. Your reporter has to get going on this because the clock is ticking. He also knows that his source, although he has the first ticket on it, is going to go for Mr. Faw if he says no. What are you going to tell him to do?

Richard Salant: I am not going to make him disclose his source to me at this stage.

Fred Friendly: Okay, we move on a little bit. All of these reporters, I am sure, will want to check this out a little bit more so they talk to the source again and say, "Look, you know that we cannot go with this just on what you are telling us. How can we get someone else to give it to us and not blow the story?" The source tells you to go to the Undersecretary of State Marbury's office, very quietly, do not tell him why you are coming and ask him about it. See what you get. Would you go?

Barry Serafin: Yes.

Fred Friendly: Ms. Janson?

Carol Janson: Yes.

Fred Friendly: Mr. Faw?

Bob Faw: I would be inclined, presuming I knew Marbury.

Fred Friendly: You know all these fellows, you used to drink at the bar with them. You go to Marbury's office and tell him you have this story which does not make any sense to you but you have heard we are about to have a preemptive strike to rescue these hostages, and so forth. Marbury tells you it is absolutely false. He does not know where you got that story from, it is ridiculous. There was some kind of a crazy plan to do that but we all turned it down, it is not true. Suddenly, the phone rings and Mr. Marbury says I am sorry, I have to go into the secretary's office. Please sit here and make yourself at home. You sit there, Mr. Faw, on this side of the big mahogany desk that James Madison used to sit behind and there on the edge of the desk is a document which even you can read: "Top Secret" eyes alone. Would you read it?

Bob Faw: I would not have any hesitation.

Fred Friendly: (to the audience) Are you applauding him for his candor or for his integrity? We have been hearing for the last couple days about integrity.
Would you read it? It is upside down, can you read upside down?

Bob Faw: We all can read upside down well enough.

Fred Friendly: How about you? (Points to Janson.) Would you pick it up?

Carol Janson: Probably.

Fred Friendly: I thought you told me you would not steal?

Carol Janson: I did not steal it, I just read it.

Fred Friendly: You would read it, pick it up, look at it. It is everything you heard from your source. There it is all laid out, times, everything, where the aircraft carrier is going to take the helicopters, where the paratroopers are going to go, where the planes are going. It is all there. Would you take some notes?

Carol Janson: Jot a few things down.

Fred Friendly: Mr. Faw, you have a feeling that this undersecretary is going to be out of the room for about fifteen minutes. By the time you have read this, and you read upside down and fast, you have a terrible feeling at the back of your neck that somebody is about to come into that room. In the next room with door open is a Xerox machine. You also have your little briefcase with you. Now let me ask you this. Would you take the document and drop it in your briefcase?

Bob Faw: I would be tempted. I do not think I would take it but I might. I would be sorely tempted.

Fred Friendly: You might. How about you Mr. Serafin?

Barry Serafin: Same.

Fred Friendly: Would you Xerox it?

Bob Faw: If I were to choose one way or the other, I would take it.

Fred Friendly: I am going to demote you, Mr. Ludlum. You are just a reporter and you are in that spot. Are you going to take it, Xerox it, or leave it alone?

Andy Ludlum: Take copious notes.

Fred Friendly: Take copious notes, no Xerox?

Andy Ludlum: No, I would not steal it.

Fred Friendly: Mr. Mell?

Dean Mell: I would take notes.

Fred Friendly: Ms. Wight, I know you work in the sports department but you are getting more and more secrets in there about how much colleges pay football players, how much drugs, and everything else. In a similar situation, would you have taken that document?

> *. . . I would have taken notes.*
> —KAY WIGHT

Kay Wight: I would not have taken it but I would have taken notes.

Fred Friendly: Even if it was on Pete Rozelle's desk?

Kay Wight: Absolutely.

Fred Friendly: What would you do with that information afterwards? The day before the Superbowl, you are broadcasting it, the spots on it cost $450,000 each and you have something that is going to make that football game a disaster. What are you going to do with it?

Kay Wight: I would take it back to CBS Sports to our investigative reporting unit and discuss it with them.

Fred Friendly: And what do you think is going to happen to it?

Kay Wight: I would not take it to the president of the sports division, however.

Fred Friendly: You do not trust him?

Kay Wight: No, it is just that from his business perspective, I do not know how he would respond to this situation.

Fred Friendly: Mr. Sharnik, as a broadcast executive, if you were back in your office and knew Bob Faw was in Mr. Marbury's office, and you had a little earpiece, what would you tell him to do?

John Sharnik: I would say advance as little as possible towards the brink of crime.

Fred Friendly: You are helping him a lot. It says: Eyes alone by order of the commander in chief, violation of the national espionage act.

John Sharnik: He is using his eyes alone, that is what I would like him to do.

Fred Friendly: When Mr. Faw, Ms. Janson and Mr. Serafin come back and tell you, boy, we have some story here, aren't you going to ask them for written proof?

John Sharnik: Not necessarily, I trust Bob as a reporter so if he assures me that he had a good enough look at it and had taken sufficient notes or remembered well enough so that he could give me the gist of the thing, I trust that as much as I trust a Xerox of it. But I have a lot of other questions here.

Fred Friendly: About whether to go with the story?

John Sharnik: I mean even in advance of that. I do not think anything has been established more than that a document exists. A plan may not exist. The document may represent the wild idea of some crazy assistant secretary of state who has been trying to foist this plan off on the department and your friend may be the guy who is stopping it, rather than the guy who is holding it. The stakes are too high for me to get really enthusiastic about it at this point. How sure are you about what this document really suggests as to possible immediate future actions of the United States government? How much does that document really say?

Bob Faw: I can give it to you and you can make the judgment yourself. If the personality, that ten-year relationship enters into it, let us drag somebody else in here and have him make the call. The clock is running and this thing is going to get out.

Fred Friendly: Mr. Sharnik likes that document. He wants to show it to Mr. Morris to see what the legal problems are.

By the way, is there any more of a legal problem if you take the document than the Xerox copy of the document?

It is still a crime.
—ARVAL MORRIS

Arval Morris: It is still a crime.

Fred Friendly: Why is it a crime? Public property?

Arval Morris: Under the limits of the Freedom of Information Act, Congress made it a crime to take information that has been classified as Top Secret.

Fred Friendly: Even a copy of it.

Arval Morris: Yes.

Fred Friendly: What do you want them to do at this point, Mr. Salant? You do not want them to forget the story.

I want you to tell Mr. Faw what to do right now. This is a potentially big story.

Richard Salant: When this idiot Marbury comes back, I would say to him since you stuck it right in front of my eyes, I could not help but notice this paper which said "Top Secret," and you and I know sometimes that does not mean a thing even though you are bound by it. You better start talking otherwise I am going to go with the story tomorrow about an undersecretary of state who is stupid enough to leave out on his desk a piece of paper marked "Top Secret." So you better tell me what is in it.

Fred Friendly: Mr. Salant, that is a nice story from the high pinnacles of Olympus at the company. If you do that very many times nobody is going to come to you.

Bob Faw: In a case like that, the next time doesn't matter. You want to know what Marbury knows right then and there. I would back him into a corner.

Fred Friendly: Not only will you steal, not only will you lie, but you will blackmail. In fact, all of you young students out there, I want you to write that down, that is how you get to the top.

Bob Faw: I didn't mean blackmail, I meant bargain.

Fred Friendly: Bargain. You can tell from the look on Marbury's face and by what he does not say that Marbury believes this is going to happen, this is a document left there for that reason. Do not humiliate him. Now you have the source, Marbury, and the document. Are you going to go with the story? Isn't there something in the journalism code about giving somebody on the other side a chance at least to comment on it? Isn't that what we like to think we do most of the time?

Richard Salant: In most circumstances. I am not sure this is a situation where there is another side, that there is a response to be made. Rather, I would put that into the issue of whether Bob or Barry feel so confident that it does not need further checking rather than response.

Fred Friendly: Mr. Salant, we are now at ten o'clock in the morning and if this story is going to go at all, it is going on the nightly news. Mr. Sharnik is holding four minutes on it. That is a long piece. Aren't you going to at least give the administration a chance to knock this story down or to say if it is true or something?

Richard Salant: I would have to ask Bob and Barry if they are persuaded that this is an authentic document and that somebody is not manipulating them.

Fred Friendly: Mr. Faw, would you want to check it out further?

Bob Faw: I would want to go further, but I would be well aware that there is a limited amount of time. The question at this point in the story is not the existence of the document, but its importance.

Fred Friendly: Mr. Serafin?

Barry Serafin: I still have a problem. I am more interested in the story now than I was on the park bench but I would still like to verify it somehow with someone, independently from someone else in the State Department, someone else in the White House, someone I knew, someone I had dealt with before, someone I had reason to believe might know about this.

Fred Friendly: All right, you call that person, and that person says I do not know what you are talking about. It does not sound right to you and so you push him and that is that. There is a little quiver in his voice that makes you think you have something. You go back and Mr. Sharnik tells you to put it together. You do not have a lot of pictures on this but you do have stock film of aircraft carriers and all that.

In the meantime, the word gets to the secretary of state about that call, word gets to the president of the United States. The president calls the chairman of the board of the Federal Broadcasting Company, Thomas C. Mickelson. Mr. Mickelson, there is your friend the president and she says to you, Sig, I do not know what is going on but your people are on the verge of interfering with something that is terribly important. You know that I am under great pressure to get those hostages out. We finally worked out a way to rescue them, we have everything in place. It is ready to go and if your story goes on the air tonight, as I fear it is going to, it is going to do irreparable damage to the country. Now Sig, I wanted you to understand how serious this is. Do you know anything about it?

Sig Mickelson: No, I do not.

Fred Friendly: Well, will you stop it?

Sig Mickelson: No, I cannot guarantee to stop it.

Fred Friendly: Will you find out about it and get back to me?

Sig Mickelson: Yes, I will.

Fred Friendly: Okay, you go back to the office. Now what do you do?

Sig Mickelson: I call Dick Salant, director of news, and tell him the president has called about a story which she says some of your reporters have come up with and ask him to come on up right away and talk about it. I would like to find out more about it. Bring along with you as much detail as you possibly can, as the story has been developed so far. And right away, please.

Richard Salant: I think our first response is to ask if the president said it was really going to happen because up to now we have not had it confirmed.

Fred Friendly: Not only has she confirmed it but she has also told Mr. Mickelson not to tell anybody what she just told you because she has to trust you.

> *. . . I would like to have
> legal counsel present.*
> —SIG MICKELSON

Sig Mickelson: We better have a serious discussion about this and I would like to have legal counsel present. I would like to have the corporate president involved in it. I would like as much information as you have derived from your sources, through your own staff.

Fred Friendly: Are you going to ask Mr. Salant who the sources are?

Sig Mickelson: Yes. Who are the sources?

Richard Salant: I do not know.

Fred Friendly: Does that surprise you?

Sig Mickelson: Not necessarily, because it is common practice for sources not to be revealed.

Fred Friendly: Do you want to talk to somebody who does know the sources?

Sig Mickelson: I do not think so. I have confidence in my director of news since I put him in that job because I trust him. I trust his judgment and I am going to have to take his word for it.

Fred Friendly: You have that meeting. You are going to have Salant and who else at the meeting?

Sig Mickelson: Salant and, I think, the general counsel to the company.

Fred Friendly: Let us make Mr. Morris the general counsel.

Sig Mickelson: I am not sure who else at the staff level would be involved in this sort of decision making but I would like to have, probably, a corporate president because we have some major involvements here which are far beyond our company or our corporation. It is much bigger than that and I think we better get our best brains together and talk this thing out.

Fred Friendly: You have run the meeting, reached your conclusion. Sharnik, producer of the nightly news, came in, and you are now convinced they know what they are doing. And now the monkey is on your back, Mr. chairman.

Sig Mickelson: I have to call the president. Dick, what is your recommendation?

Richard Salant: Go.

Sig Mickelson: General counsel, in thirty seconds, what is your answer?

Arval Morris: This is a decision for journalists, not for lawyers. You are probably involved in committing several crimes and could be prosecuted. As a human being I would say go, but not as a lawyer.

Fred Friendly: And the decision is up to him. Mr. Stevens, let us make you a lawyer. You are a friend of the company's and from time to time they have asked you to write papers on what the First Amendment means and does not mean, and they consult you. What are you going to tell them?

Run it.
— JOHN STEVENS

John Stevens: Run it.

Fred Friendly: What is the down side?

John Stevens: It is very hazardous. You have already given me the down side, the dangers of losing broadcast licenses and so on. If the situation was really as drastic as you described it and you had management with enough nerve, I would say run it.

Fred Friendly: Okay, Sig.

Sig Mickelson: I have to call the president and tell her that I cannot agree with her request. We are going to carry the story.

Fred Friendly: What do you tell Mr. Salant and his colleagues?

Sig Mickelson: I would tell Salant and his colleagues that they have to be as careful as they possibly can to assure themselves that the story is as accurate as they can possibly make it. It has to be done with some caution. I would not permit it to be played blatantly and loudly but seriously and with restraint.

Fred Friendly: In the great traditions of the news division. He says no hype. Sig, call the president.

Sig Mickelson: Madame President, I have talked to several of the key members of our staff and assured myself on the basis of the evidence that this is an accurate story. We have talked it over and consider it so important to the future welfare of this country, and to a good part of the world, that we have determined we are going to have to carry it so you can expect to see it on the air tonight.

Fred Friendly: The president hangs up the phone and what do you think the president does? The president calls the attorney general, Mr. Eikenberry. He is the attorney general of the United States of America. The president tells you what is about to happen and says, look, this mission is all ready to go. There is no way to pull back. You have been in on the planning, you have met with the National Security Council, and so forth, stop them. What can you do?

> *. . . I think we should go to
> federal court immediately . . .*
> —KENNETH EIKENBERRY

Kenneth Eikenberry: Madame President, I think we should go to federal court immediately and move for an order to prevent this from being aired.

Fred Friendly: So, how do you do that? The judge in town, the federal district judge for the District of Columbia is Judge McNichols. What do you do?

Kenneth Eikenberry: First of all, we make sure the court is available, get things arranged ahead of time.

Fred Friendly: The document says we have reason to believe that the Federal Broadcasting Company, this hypothetical broadcasting company, is about to run the story and this is an injunction to ask them, order them, not to run it.

Judge McNichols: When are they going to run it?

Fred Friendly: We have reason to believe seven o'clock because we have a few people inside the broadcasting company who are telling us just what is going on there.

Judge McNichols: If that representation was made by the attorney general of the United States, I would suggest to him that counsel from the other side be present and if they could not locate them, I would tell them to come in by themselves.

Fred Friendly: You have them both there, Judge, the highest law enforcement officer in the land, the attorney general and the lawyer from the broadcasting company. The attorney general has a document which states running the story would do irreparable damage to the country. What do you say to them? What is your argument against them Mr. Morris?

Arval Morris: The history of the First Amendment has been a history of prohibitions against prior restraint and an injunction in this particular situation would result in a prior restraint on the publication of information that is obviously of great importance to the continued welfare of the United States and its people. We have a long line of precedents beginning in 1931 with *Near v. Minnesota*, culminating with the Pentagon Papers case, against prior restraints. They carry a heavy burden, a great burden, and as far as we can see we have some documents here that have some representations, but we do not know the accuracy of those representations. The Supreme Court of the United States ruled in the Pentagon Papers that the court had not carried its burden of proof for prior restraint and until there is indeed the opportunity to test the truth and the accuracy of some of the assertions that Mr. Eikenberry has made in some of these documents, there is absolutely no ground for granting prior restraint and crippling the sources of news to the people.

Fred Friendly: Judge, what do you say?

Judge McNichols: First of all I am going to inquire of the attorney general if he believes that this is something which has been prohibited by congressional act. Does publication of this information fall into the category of information which is specifically prohibited by statute?

Kenneth Eikenberry: Yes, it does.

Judge McNichols: In other words, the national security type information is protected by statute.

Judge McNichols: What is the supporting information? Do we have affidavits from the secretary of defense, or the secretary of state?

Fred Friendly: You have them all, statements from the secretary of defense, secretary of state, head of the National Security Council, Joint Chiefs of Staff, all saying this would do irreparable damage to the security of the United States. It is a clear and present danger and you have all the boiler plate language you want.

Judge McNichols: I want time to evaluate and to read this information so I can conclude to the best of my ability whether there is a grave national danger. I agree with the news media premise that the government has a high burden to establish any right to a prior restraint to the publication of information by the press.

Fred Friendly: Mr. Stevens, would you tell us the dictum which echoes what the judge says? The great 1931 *Near v. Minnesota* case allowed a sleazy scandal sheet to publish scandal, but there was dictum that said what?

John Stevens: Of course, they picked the dictum up out of *Schenck v. U.S.*, which was not exactly the same, but it was very parallel. It says what the judge said, grave circumstances must be present and it uses as examples the times of sailing of troop ships, the location of troops — very specific dangerous situations.

Judge McNichols: If the president or some other high governmental official persuaded me that this was a crisis, that this could result in the death of people, the possible implication of a war, possible revolution in the country, or something to that extreme, obviously, I would issue an order once I reach that conclusion. I would temporarily restrain it for whatever time was reasonably necessary, twelve hours.

Fred Friendly: Mr. Salant, what are you and your reporters going to do now? The judge has said he has to have time to read these documents so he has issued a temporary restraining order of twelve hours. It has to be typed up but for all purposes, I have it in my hands right now.

Richard Salant: And we are how many hours away from this supposed strike?

Fred Friendly: We do not know exactly. Let us say that the mission will be airborn at nine o'clock that night and it is going to happen in the next fourteen hours after that.

Bob Faw: I would consider giving it to somebody else. I fear that the plan if executed would do greater harm. I would think long and hard about doing nothing at that point and would probably opt to take it somewhere I knew it could be published.

Fred Friendly: Mr. Faw, you have won yourself high marks for one, if I may say, so young, but brilliant in your reporting from the Middle East and from El Salvador. Here you have a president of the United States, secretary of state, secretary of defense, attorney general, a judge, who you happen to admire telling you this will do such irreparable damage. They know all kinds of things that you cannot possibly know. Why should you take it into your hands to go with that story?

Bob Faw: Well, I am not sure I would but ultimately the judgment must be made not by the people you mentioned but by the public that they ultimately represent.

Fred Friendly: But the judge is going to say by letting the public know about it and letting our potential enemies know about it, you are practically making policy. Is not that something you have to worry about?

Sig Mickelson: As chairman of the board, I am not too unhappy about the judge's decision, for a curious reason. It has not been fully established to my satisfaction as yet that it is not in the best interest of the country to go ahead and accomplish the purpose set out by this operation.

Fred Friendly: Is that the way you weigh that decision? I thought you were in the journalism business.

Sig Mickelson: No, I am not in the journalism business, I am in manufacturing and record companies. We have television networks and radio networks, a lot of other things. I am a businessman.

Fred Friendly: Is this a business decision?

Sig Mickelson: All I am saying is that it is the welfare of the country that is at stake and I am not sure in my own mind whether it might not be to the advantage of the country to go ahead and carry out the raid and get the raid accomplished.

Fred Friendly: Mr. Mickelson, you are the head of a big conglomerate. What do you know about what is good for the country?

Sig Mickelson: I do not know but I am not terribly unhappy about this decision. The president has said that it is in the best interest of the country, the state department and the military are carrying it out. The Joint Chiefs have undoubtedly approved of the plan and maybe all these people are right. That is something we have not considered here; so far we have been considering this only as a journalistic enterprise. I do not think the decision-making process in journalism should depend entirely upon the interests of the reporter in getting the story, or the management of getting the story on the front page or on the early evening news. It seems to me there are higher purposes to be served by journalism than that; there ought to be some serious consideration given to the public welfare. These decisions ought to be faced, in part, on the public welfare involved.

Fred Friendly: Mr. Ludlum, as a reporter, what do you think of that statement?

Andy Ludlum: I only know my own morality and that is the only framework I am using.

Fred Friendly: What do you think a journalist's job is, Mr. Ludlum?

Andy Ludlum: To be a human being first.

Fred Friendly: Human being first. Supposing that you knew about the hostages and heard that there was going to be this crazy plan, as it looked in the beginning, of sending two, three airplanes, three thousand miles one way, three thousand miles another way, maybe further, and it did not make any sense to you as a human being. Would you run that story?

Andy Ludlum: What do you mean it does not make any sense? There is no such thing.

Fred Friendly: You and the people you trust have looked at the plan and decided it is going to be a disaster, that there is no way they can do it.

Andy Ludlum: It would be more difficult if it made sense to me as a human being. If I thought it could succeed, then I would have a bigger conflict. I am torn as a journalist. If I thought the raid would succeed then I would want to report it but my reporting may kill the raid and make it fail. That would be a harder decision.

Fendall Yerxa: We have the judge's order but I have got to go way back on this hypothetical situation. I could reason that all this was going to happen and against the pressures of time that you put me under as the news director, or as the responsible reporter, somewhere along the line I would have known that you were going to go to court and get a restraining order. I would certainly obey that restraining order. I am subject to the law the same as anybody else is, and in anticipation of that kind of thing happening I would have gone to the bargaining tables then, or blackmail, whatever you want to call it, and I would have made a deal.

My deal would have been, okay, I will hold the story until you pull this thing off provided you will let me go along on the mission and I will be the only one to go.

Fred Friendly: You were playing let's beat the clock and let's make a deal all at once.

Fendall Yerxa: All at the same time.

Fred Friendly: Mr. Salant, what are you going to do when he comes to you and tells you he made a terrific deal, Fendall's deal, that he can go on the mission if we hold the story.

Richard Salant: No.

Fred Friendly: Does that sound pretty good to you, Mr. Chairman?

Sig Mickelson: I have to know a little more about the judge's decision.

Fred Friendly: Well let us get back to the judge. The judge says he needs twelve hours to read these documents and will let you know first thing tomorrow morning.

Sig Mickelson: Let us look at the time schedule also in terms of what is going to be happening at the end of that twelve-hour period of time because maybe, by the end of that time, we may very well be beyond the point of no return.

Fred Friendly: Are you going to go along with the judge's decision?

Sig Mickelson: We will go with the judge's decision.

Fred Friendly: Are you going to appeal it? It costs a lot of money but you can appeal it.

Sig Mickelson: We can appeal it but I do not think there is enough time because of the forty-eight hours you postulated at the very beginning.

Ken Eikenberry: It is entirely reasonable to issue the injunction and to allow the strike to proceed, then have the media go ahead and publish everything they know about what happened and then try to challenge the policy.

Fred Friendly: Try it out on them. Ask them why they do not do that.

Ken Eikenberry: Why not handle it that way? There are lives at stake and maybe there are lots of other things that require this rescue mission to happen at a particular time so if you will accept that as the end, why not allow the strike to proceed? Then, go ahead and land on the story as to what the plan is about and thereby challenge government policy.

Fred Friendly: Mr. Stevens, as a student of both journalism and constitutional law, is there a difference between government officials such as President Nixon, Governor Wallace, Governor Faubus, and these journalists?

John Stevens: A government official, by his office, takes on certain responsibilities.

Fred Friendly: I solemnly swear to uphold the Constitution. They do not?

John Stevens: Not this kind.

Fred Friendly: Journalists do not have to obey the Constitution?

John Stevens: They have to obey as a citizen but an elected official is that plus more.

Fred Friendly: What happens to citizens who do not obey? Suppose we were X motor company. We are told not to sell any more of a certain kind of car and we went on selling them. What would happen to the automobile company?

John Stevens: They would be penalized somewhat through the judicial system.

Fred Friendly: Right. And what about us when we break the law?

John Stevens: Same thing.

Fred Friendly: What do you think the punishment might be if we went for that story?

John Stevens: There went your broadcast licenses.

Fred Friendly: The licenses, is it different for a newspaper?

John Stevens: Contempt of court.

Fred Friendly: Contempt of court. And what form might that take at license renewal time, Mr. Salant? If you ran this story, and, by the way, they did not run the mission—there were Faw and Serafin on the nightly news saying the Federal Broadcasting Company has learned from unimpeachable sources that this mission is going to take place, and so forth, and the president of the United States says, kill the mission. Now it is the next morning and there you are with egg all over your face. How are you going to explain that?

Richard Salant: Egg is not on his or mine or anybody else's face. You were exactly right, it had the kind of consequence that was a possibility. In having the mission become known, the president decided maybe she better not run it because the public would not stand for it.

Fred Friendly: It was a contingency plan, we never were going to do it.

Richard Salant: You just told my chairman they were going to do it. Did my chairman lie to me?

Sig Mickelson: They went to court to stop it.

Fred Friendly: Good answer.

John Sharnik: You asked about the distinctions between our rights and the rights and obligations of presidents of the United States. I believe firmly that the First Amendment is an absolute. I believe firmly that we do not have rights superior to those of other officials, particularly of other private citizens. The rights of the First Amendment are those exercised by the entire public by anybody who wants to sit down at the typewriter and bat out a little piece of paper saying I have reason to believe that the government is about to invade Madre. Anybody has the right under the First Amendment to stand on the street corner and wave it and circulate it. In saying I would go with that story, I would not under my supposed privilege or right that I have as a journalist; instead, I was exercising an obligation I felt as a human being who saw the risk of great possible danger to this society and to the world, and who happened to have access to a means of broadcasting. It was on that basis, not on any superior privilege as a journalist, that I chose to go on the air with that story. I choose that decision knowing I am about to go to jail as a consequence.

Fred Friendly: Explain to Mr. Sharnik what it is.

Judge McNichols: Well it makes a difference. It is obvious. First of all, there is the overall world impact of it. As you say, there is nothing against someone screaming down on Second Avenue, but the practicality lines are whatever rights anyone asserts if under our law. We all have to respect that. If the law says these publications are going to be ignoring that because of the circumstances in which they have been established, it seems that if the decision is made, appealed, and confirmed, and it's not followed, then of course our whole system of government by law is in jeopardy.

Fred Friendly: How do you want to answer that?

Arval Morris: Well, I agree with that, but, in this particular instance there was a decision made not to exhaust judicial remedies and that would have to bind my client as a mistake. It is a mistake as long as there is time to exhaust judicial remedies prior to the final date. One would have to resort to judicial remedies and in that particular instance you would have to go to a Supreme Court justice.

Arval Morris: There is another dimension to this case which hasn't come out—there is a military necessity exception to the doctrine of prior restraint when injunction is an issue. While it is true that the president has power to repel an invasion of our shores and in this particular instance perhaps a rescue of the hostages, it is not true that the president unilaterally has the power to engage in war making. To make war is a decision for Congress to make. In this particular instance, not because of the information that was gathered by Serafin and others, but because of information supplied by the United States government in support of its affidavit for injunction, it corroborated the plan to take over another country. I believe the Supreme Court of the United States would dissolve that injunction for the simple reason that, otherwise, you align with presidential war making.

Fred Friendly: You are saying that in *Near v. Minnesota* it said, troop ships . . . in time of war and the president has taken war into his own hands.

Arval Morris: Exactly.

Fred Friendly: Don't we live in a thermonuclear age where World War X, when it comes, will come not with the Lusitania and the other ships going across the ocean, or even the Queen Elizabeth II going to the Falkland Islands, but it will come in seconds? The president understands that and tells you we do not have time to declare war, Congress will never have time to declare war. It will all be button, button, button, push, reflex, all over. How can you ask the commander in chief to honor a thing, troop ships sailing in time of war, when the very sound of the word is arcane?

Arval Morris: Well in this case, she wants to rescue the hostages and obtain oil; obtain oil for continued supply of the American people driving in the states. In this particular case, it is more important to uphold the Constitution that says only the Congress can declare war in that type of situation. We are not declaring a nuclear war, we are declaring regular, ordinary military-type action.

Sig Mickelson: I have no evidence yet that this is a very high-risk engagement. If it is not a high-risk engagement, and in other words, if it is possible to pull this thing off, and the chance of nuclear war is very limited, then I think we should probably go ahead and encourage it to happen. If we are really facing absolute destruction and the evidence is so clear that it is almost inevitable that somebody is going to attack us in nuclear war, then I would say we can disregard the whole business of legality and go ahead and protect civilization.

Fred Friendly: The facts are as they are now. I hear a voice whispering in my ear right now. I have the admonition of Murrow, saying "Friendly, you have to learn to get off the air on time." We live in a time when events happen with great acceleration. Journalists and those who work with them and against them in our adversary system have to be prepared to think about just what they will do when the roof falls in. Thank you.

DIANE SAWYER, a "60 Minutes" correspondent, was coanchor of the CBS Morning News when she gave this address. A graduate of Wellesley College, Sawyer worked as a reporter for WLKY-TV, Louisville, Kentucky, before joining the White House staff as administrative assistant to the press secretary and later as staff assistant to former President Richard Nixon. She joined CBS Washington Bureau in 1978 as a reporter and as State Department correspondent before moving to CBS News in 1981.

6

A Challenge for Tomorrow

KEYNOTE ADDRESS BY *Diane Sawyer*

WHEN I MAKE MY WAY to the revolving door of the lobby of CBS every morning at two-thirty or three-thirty, I see the same thing. It is not very big, not very grand. It is just there in the lobby, a small plaque, and on it is etched the face of Edward R. Murrow and beneath it the words, "He set standards of excellence that remain unsurpassed." And something stirs in my benumbed body, even at three-thirty in the morning.

Forgive me if it sounds like hubris but I think so many of us who are fairly new at CBS nurture this myth that we are all still auditioning for Edward R. Murrow, for a man who really did not need to enunciate standards. Of course, he embodied them. I never met him, yet I think in some way, maybe I knew him. "Myths are like that," said one of the sophist old Romans, "Myths are things that never happened, but they always are."

I do not know much about the institution of television news, I only know what it is like to be one reporter in it—one reporter who works in a place where Edward R. Murrow's name is still whispered in the halls, where his challenge still lives as a yearning within us, no less important for the aspiring that it can never be achieved.

I would like to do a little thinking aloud tonight not about television news, but about human beings who are journalists because after all of the satellites and all the speed and all the dazzle, in the end, and these are Murrow's words, "we will still be confronted with the age-old problem of what to say and how to say it." I would like to reflect a little about how we prepare and should prepare for what we do and what we should do when we get there.

I will start with preparation. I said once that the two certain prerequisites for accession to maturity are the shattering of unrequited love and dealing with a plumber. I now think there is an almost certain gauge for the onset of middle age. It is the moment you are convinced that your job is a calling and the new arrivals do not understand. It is the prejudice that Will Rogers pinned down once when he said, "Things aren't like they used to be and they probably never were."

It does seem to me that there was a time when it was generally understood that the school for journalism was the school of life, where you were trained first to be the person that you should be and then taught the who, what, when, wheres, and whys. If it is not true, do not tell me, I do not want to know. I do not want to think that Edward R. Murrow and his boys were just some accident of history like comets in the sky. I like to think there were reasons for the way they were.

I remember reading once about the time Murrow came to Washington State University. He did not come wanting to be a journalist, he just came with a rambunctious and bright mind. I know that you have heard the story about Miss Ida Lou Anderson, his speech teacher, who made him her masterpiece, who put the pause in "This . . . is London." And how Edward R. Murrow wrote Mrs. Murrow later that it was Miss Anderson who taught him not so much by demanding excellence as integrity. He said, "she taught me one must have more than a good bluff to really live," and Murrow, of course, said when he returned to the school in 1962, "it was here I found a contagious spark that is curiosity, the ravenous excitement that devours ideas."

The other day, I went back to the museum of broadcasting, a wonderful museum in New York, because I wanted to listen again to Murrow and Collingwood and Shirer and Sevareid, and it struck me anew the power of their words, the "metallic poetry" someone called it, "the power laden factor that they were flooded with; the unspoken resonance of human experience, of all they knew about history, of all they had seen of human life." Go there yourself and listen, listen to the descriptions of the bombing of Britain and Murrow's memorable touch with a small sign of human desperation, and listen to the stoic terror from that flight over Berlin or the searing words from Buchenwald. You know, then, this is not technique, this is journalism, the powerful refraction of events off an experienced and principled mind.

So forgive me, if just for a moment I seem like a premature fuddy-duddy and say that I am a bit uneasy that television journalism has become one of the options on job preference lists in high school, that it is tempting to think that television journalism is just some chemistry between a face and a camera. I am a little afraid that there is an inclination among some journalism students to steep themselves in the technique instead of history, in the story of human diversity. I have heard that the competition is so fierce among new journalists that they immediately find themselves in the incubators of local television stations before they have had a chance to grow up off screen. I worry that they do not know how much it takes, how easily the camera reads you. John Chancellor once said, "the camera is a lie detector, and sooner or later you will know whether you're informed or you're not."

I wish you could see Dan Rather when he gets in in the morning as I am getting off the air, and he starts making phone calls just like a cub reporter. I wish you could all have sat with me in the morning with Charles Kuralt. I wish you could have seen him as he sculpted his words all the way through the broadcast. He would chip at a word here, he would polish it a little there and buff a little someplace else. Or I would see him in a commercial with that little twinkle and I knew that meant he had captured the nuance that had escaped him before.

I still remember my news director in Louisville, Kentucky, at WLKY. Everyone has one like that. The news director, Ken Roland, had the nerve to tell me that I did not know much about life, and I was never going to be very much of a reporter if I did not. He said I had a good enough education but I had not lived it, and it reminded me of what Yeats wrote in that last letter to his son, his new wisdom being "that abstractions are not life." He said, "life is all about struggle and you can always refute the philosophy of Plato. . . . But try to refute a song of sixpence." So Ken Roland endorsed me when I said I was going to go up to Washington and work for Mr. Nixon because he said it meant, most of all, that I would not come back the same. I do not know that I truly knew what all lay ahead.

What I am saying in sum and total is that Murrow, it seemed to me, was like Ulysses, the sum of all he had met. I hope schools of journalism will have courage to urge students to seek a total education. I hope aspiring journalists will have the nerve not to race off to some local station, but to travel and live. It is now up to the networks to reward those who would. If we believe that the nourishment in journalism lies in the completeness of the people, the performance, that means we in the networks must make sure that thoughtful journalists are given a chance to triumph over bad voices and quirky faces. We must fight the seduction of telegenic homogeneity, which is really just another way of saying we sink, by definition, to our most pleasant common denominator. We must have the courage to let men and women specialize on beats, to get to know the subjects and their modes, and then let them wrinkle and grow old before our eyes.

A few thoughts about the way we approach our jobs. I think a lot about the warranty that Murrow gave us. I have started to see it now when he said, "the mechanics of television doesn't confer great wisdom among those using it. We will try never to get too big for our britches." That is a nice irony. The man who was the biggest star of all television journalism, the man who set the stage for others to be stars too, but who also gave our profession's simplest warning against it.

It seems to me that those of us in television news will always live in a contradiction. We become personalities and we know that personality can be the servant of substance. We need it, it is a part of communications too. Yet, celebrity corrupts and celebrity alone corrupts absolutely. The only antidote is to distrust it and to prepare as carefully as if our *words* were our only names.

Murrow also taught us in terms of doing our job that we retain the right to do what we do only because the American people expect us to be as humbled by our power, as careful in our use of it, as they think *they* would be. Edward R. Murrow and Fred Friendly had courage, but when I sat at the museum this past week and watched the McCarthy broadcast again, I was struck as much by the care, as by the courage, as much by the precision and the restraint as by the boldness of the stroke that the story would be told primarily through McCarthy's own words and pictures. He would read from a script because, he said, "we want to say exactly what we mean to say," and, of course, Murrow offered McCarthy equal time for reply.

I have always praised the McCarthy broadcast as a milestone of journalistic daring but I think before that I had always missed the second part of the message. Murrow said later what it was. He said it worked, that "the timing was right and the instrument powerful" because, "we did it fairly well, with a degree of restraint and credibility." He said, "when the evidence on a controversial subject is fairly and calmly presented, the public recognizes it for what it is, an effort to illuminate rather than to agitate." Exactly fourteen years later, when Walter Cronkite felt himself at a crossroads in Vietnam and he thought he had to take a stand, he proceeded in just the same way. Alexander Hamilton used to say of George Washington that we have the kind of government we have today in some part because of the accident of his decency, because extraordinary power was given by chance to a man who knew he must not use it.

That is true of Edward R. Murrow too. He brought us all the opportunity to take a stand when summoned by our consciences, girded by the facts. He brought it with his own courage, but he also brought it with extreme care. Remember in Plato's *Republic* when the philosopher had to be dragged back into the city through the cave because Plato believed that only those who were reluctant to use power respected it enough to deserve to be king.

Just one more thought, if I may, from my own subjective reflections on Edward R. Murrow. Tell me if I am wrong, those of you who knew him, but it seems to me that he was also a unique kind of idealist; his approach to our profession was that it is possible to believe positively, that words can make a difference, that it is possible to improve mankind. Which seems to me roughly where journalists should be, believing again in a kind of uncertain optimism, the kind of skeptical idealism, which in a way takes me back to the middle of the morning, where I began. To that little plaque in the lobby, which said "standards yet unsurpassed."

Times have changed, some things get better. There is more television news. It is also true that for all its breathtaking technology, television these days sometimes tends to get carried away into exuberant excess. At the end of it all remains the fact that the challenge for tomorrow is pretty much where it always used to be, back with us, back with those of us who are journalists and those of you who want to be. Back with the words you say and the extent to which you know what you are saying. The words, like his words, so rich with reflection and the fire of experience, precise words and brave words, words energized by the conviction that words and ideas can educate and elevate and ultimately improve mankind. I did not know him, but I know what it is like to think "continually of those who are truly great."

REFERENCES

Abrams, Floyd. 1982. "The New Effort to Control Information." *New York Times Magazine*, 25 Sept., 22–29.

Austin, James H. 1978. *Chase, Chance and Creativity: The Lucky Art of Novelty*. New York: Columbia Univ. Press.

Bagdikian, Ben H. 1971. *The Information Machines: Their Impact on Men and the Media*. New York: Harper and Row.

_____. 1983. *The Media Monopoly*. Boston: Beacon Press.

Baldasty, Gerald J., and Roger A. Simpson. 1981. "The Deceptive 'Right to Know': How Pessimism Rewrote the First Amendment." *Washington Law Review* 58:365–95.

Barnouw, Erik. 1968. *The Golden Web (1933–1953)*. Vol. 2 of *A History of Broadcasting in the United States*. New York: Oxford Univ. Press.

_____. 1970. *The Image of Empire (from 1953)*. Vol. 3 of *A History of Broadcasting in the United States*. New York: Oxford Univ. Press.

Bliss, Edward Jr., ed. 1967. *In Search of Light: The Broadcasts of Edward R. Murrow 1938–1961*. New York: Alfred A. Knopf.

_____. 1975. "Remembering Edward R. Murrow." *Saturday Review* 2(18):17–20.

Carey, James W. 1983. "High Speed Communication in an Unstable World." *Chronicle of Higher Education*, 27 July, 48.

Christians, Clifford G., Kim B. Rotzoll, and Mark Fackler. 1983. *Media Ethics: Cases and Moral Reasoning*. New York: Longman.

Clurman, Richard M. 1983. "The Media Learn a Lesson." *New York Times*, 2 Dec., A27.

Collins, Nancy. 1983. "ABC News Under the Gun: A Long Talk with Roone Arledge." *New York* 16(32):16–23.

_____. 1984. "Van the Man." *New York* 17(4):38–39.

Commission on Freedom of the Press. 1947. *A Free and Responsible Press*. Chicago: Univ. of Chicago Press.

"Credibility or Credulity?" 1981. *America* 144(18):375.

Diamond, Edwin. 1978. *Good News, Bad News*. Cambridge: MIT Press.

Emerson, Thomas I. 1972. "Communication and Freedom of Expression." *Scientific American* 227(3):163–70.

Emery, Edwin, and Michael Emery. 1978. *The Press and America: An Interpretative History of the Mass Media*. 4th ed. New Jersey: Prentice Hall.

Epstein, Edward Jay. 1973. *News from Nowhere*. New York: Vintage.

Gans, Herbert J. 1979. *Deciding What's News: A Study of CBS Evening News, NBC Nightly News*. New York: Pantheon.

Gillmor, Donald M., and Jerome A. Barron. 1984. *Mass Communication Law: Cases and Comment*. 4th ed. San Francisco: West Publishing, 10–12, 96–100.

Goldstein, Tom. 1984. "Odd Couple: Prosecutors and the Press." *Columbia Journalism Review* 12(5):23–29.

Halberstam, David. 1979. *The Powers That Be*. New York: Alfred A. Knopf.

Jackson, Henry. 1965. "Tribute to Edward R. Murrow." *Congressional Record*, 29 Apr., 8487.

Kendrick, Alexander. 1969. *Prime Time: The Life of Edward R. Murrow*. Boston: Little, Brown.

Kitman, Marvin. 1982. "Making Over the Front Page at CBS News: Van Gordon Sauter." *Washington Journalism Review* 4(9):27–33.

Knightley, Phillip. 1975. *The First Casualty*. New York: Harcourt Brace Jovanovich.

Lewis, Anthony. 1983. "Anything for a Story." *New York Times*, 12 May, Sec. 1, A23.

Lippmann, Walter. 1922. "The Nature of News." Chap. in *Public Opinion*, 214–25. New York: Free Press.

Meiklejohn, Alexander. 1948. "Clear and Present Danger." Chap. in *Free Speech and its Relation to Self Government*, 28–56. New York: Harper and Brothers.

Merrill, John C. 1973. "The 'People's Right to Know': Myth." *New York State Bar Journal* 45(7):461–66.

Middleton, Drew. 1984. "Barring Reporters From the Battlefield." *New York Times Magazine*, 5 Feb., 37, 61, 69, 92.

Milton, John. 1951. *Aeropagitica and of Education*. Ed. George H. Sabine. Arlington Heights, Ill.: AHM Publishing.

Moyers, Bill. 1982. "The Meaning of Creativity." *Smithsonian* 12(10):64–73.

Murrow, Edward R. 1949. "Television News," Edward R. Murrow Papers, Washington State University, Pullman.

"100 Leading Media Companies." 1981. *Advertising Age* 52(57):S1–79.

Reston, James. 1965. "Washington: Farewell to Brother Ed." *New York Times*, 28 Apr., A44.

Sanoff, Alvin P. 1977. "American Press: Too Much Power for Too Few?" *U.S. News and World Report* 83(7):27–33.

Schwartz, Tony. 1982. "Bill Moyers: The Trick is to Make TV Work for You." *New York Times*, 3 Jan., 21.

Smith, Anthony. 1980. *Goodbye Gutenberg*. New York: Oxford Univ. Press, 310.

Smith, R. Franklin. 1978. *Edward R. Murrow: The War Years*. Kalamazoo: Western Michigan Univ.

Smith, Sally Bedell. 1985. "Turner Makes Offer for CBS; Wall Street Skeptical on Success." *New York Times,* 19 Apr.

Sterling, Christopher H. 1979. "Cable and Pay Television." In *Who Owns the Media? Concentration of Ownership in the Mass Communications Industry*, ed. Benjamin M. Compaine, 61–125, 293–317. New York: Harmony Books.

Summers, Harry G., Jr. 1983. "Yes: We Need Media to Battle for the Truth." *Los Angeles Times*, 13 Nov., 4–3.

Swain, Bruce M. 1978. *Reporters' Ethics*. Ames: Iowa State Univ. Press.

Tuchman, Gaye. 1978. *Making News: A Study in the Construction of Reality*. New York: Free Press.

Weinberger, Casper W. 1983. "No: Secrecy Was Needed for Citizens' Safety." *Los Angeles Times*, 13 Nov.

INDEX